Fourth Grade Math
with Confidence
Student Workbook
Part A

Fourth Grade Math
with Confidence

Student Workbook

Part A

KATE SNOW

WELL-TRAINED MIND PRESS

Names: Snow, Kate (Teacher), author.

Title: Fourth grade math with confidence. Student workbook part A / Kate Snow.

Other titles: Student workbook part A

Description: [Charles City, Virginia] : Well-Trained Mind Press, [2024] | Series: Math with confidence | Interest age level: 009-010.

Identifiers: ISBN: 978-1-944481-52-0 (paperback)

Subjects: LCSH: Mathematics--Study and teaching (Elementary) | LCGFT: Problems and exercises. | BISAC: JUVENILE NONFICTION / MATHEMATICS / Arithmetic.

Classification: LCC: QA107.2 .S664 2024 | DDC: 372.7--dc23

1 2 3 4 5 6 7 8 9   Mercury   30 29 28 27 26 25 24

Table of Contents

Author's Note

You'll need three books to teach *Fourth Grade Math with Confidence.* All three books are essential for the program.

- The Instructor Guide contains the scripted lesson plans for the entire year (Units 1-16).
- Student Workbook Part A contains the workbook pages for the first half of the year (Units 1-8).
- Student Workbook Part B contains the workbook pages for the second half of the year (Units 9-16).

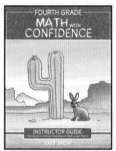  

The Student Workbooks are not meant to be used as stand-alone workbooks. The hands-on teaching activities in the Instructor Guide are an essential part of the program. You'll need the directions in the Instructor Guide to guide your child through the Lesson Activities pages. The icon with two heads means that your child should complete these pages with you, and that she is not expected to complete these pages on her own.

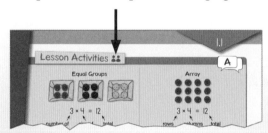

The Practice and Review pages give your child practice with new concepts and review previously-learned skills. The icon with one head means that your child may complete these pages on his own. Most fourth-graders will be able to complete these workbook pages independently, but some may need help reading and interpreting the directions.

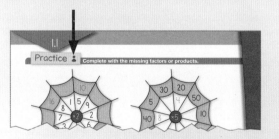 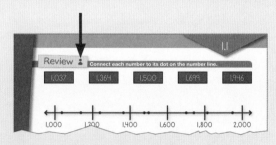

Lesson Activities 👥

Equal Groups

$$3 \times 4 = 12$$

number of groups   size of each group   total

Array

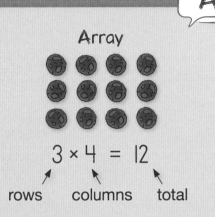

$$3 \times 4 = 12$$

rows   columns   total

$$3 \times 4 = 12$$

factors   product

Climb and Slide

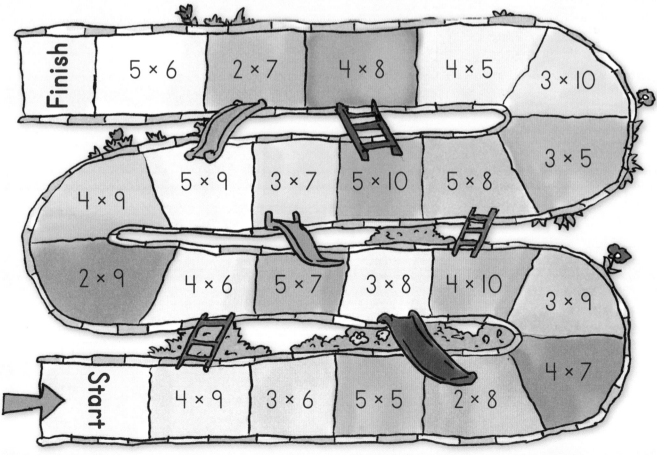

Finish

| 5 × 6 | 2 × 7 | 4 × 8 | 4 × 5 | 3 × 10 |

3 × 5

| 4 × 9 | 5 × 9 | 3 × 7 | 5 × 10 | 5 × 8 |

| 2 × 9 | 4 × 6 | 5 × 7 | 3 × 8 | 4 × 10 |

3 × 9

4 × 7

Start

| 4 × 9 | 3 × 6 | 5 × 5 | 2 × 8 |

Practice 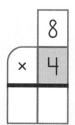 Complete with the missing factors or products.

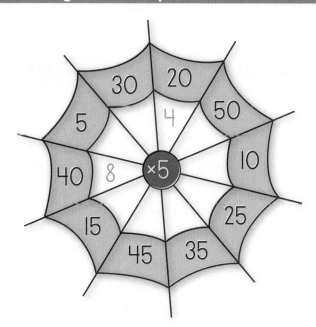

Complete.

	8
×	4

	9
×	5

	2
×	7

	3
×	8

	4
×	9

Review 👤

Connect each number to its dot on the number line.

| 1,037 | 1,364 | 1,500 | 1,699 | 1,946 |

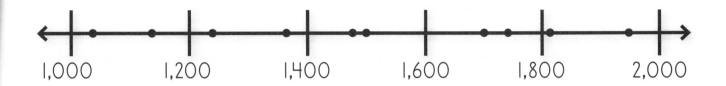

1,000   1,200   1,400   1,600   1,800   2,000

| 1,137 | 1,239 | 1,475 | 1,740 | 1,812 |

Write the number that comes before and after each number.

79	80	81

	99	

	347	

	2,694	

	999	

	5,000	

Complete with <, >, or =.

40 + 7 ◯ 40 + 8

40 − 7 ◯ 40 − 8

30 + 6 ◯ 6 + 30

200 + 5 ◯ 500 + 2

Match pairs that equal 500.

400	250
300	100
250	350
150	200

Lesson Activities 👥

Multiples of 6	6	12	18	24	30	36	42	48	54	60
Multiples of 7	7	14	21		35	42		56	63	70
Multiples of 8	8		24		40		56		72	
Multiples of 9	9			45					90

B

$7 \times 9 =$ ☐ $8 \times 8 =$ ☐ $6 \times 9 =$ ☐

C

Multiples Four in a Row

64	49	42	72	36
63	36	48	81	56
48	42	54	56	48
56	81	63	42	64
54	36	72	49	54

Practice

Complete the missing numbers in the mixed-up multiplication charts. Then, use the charts to answer the questions.

×	3	6	2	10	8	1	9			
2	6	12				2	18	10	14	8

×	2	10	1			7		9	6	
3	6	30	3	24	15		12			9

×	5	6		1		2		10		9
4	20		12		32		16		28	

×	8		3		4		1		5	
5		35		50		30		45		10

Is 10 a multiple of 2?	Is 10 a multiple of 3?
Is 15 a multiple of 3?	Is 15 a multiple of 5?
Is 16 a multiple of 4?	Is 16 a multiple of 2?
Is 20 a multiple of 2?	Is 20 a multiple of 3?
Is 20 a multiple of 4?	Is 20 a multiple of 5?

Review

Color the multiples in order from Start to End.

Multiples of 6

END

8	10	14	56	60
6	12	15	48	54
21	18	25	42	45
20	24	30	36	40
25	27	32	52	39

Start

Multiples of 7

14	21	28	35	48
7	25	32	42	49
12	15	40	54	56
16	18	30	60	63
24	20	81	72	70

Start

END

Circle the odd numbers. X the even numbers.

73   978   1,000

456   45   9,732

1,374   8,643   2,001

Complete.

$ _____

$ _____

Complete each blank with the greatest possible number.

3 × [2] < 8   4 × [ ] < 10   5 × [ ] < 11

4 × [ ] < 13   7 × [ ] < 15   6 × [ ] < 16

6 × [ ] < 20   4 × [ ] < 21   3 × [ ] < 25

Lesson Activities 👥

12 children split into groups of 4.
How many groups do they make?

$12 \div 4 = \boxed{}$

↑ total   ↑ size of each group   ↑ number of groups

12 children split into 4 equal groups.
How many children are in each group?

$12 \div 4 = \boxed{}$

↑ total   ↑ number of groups   ↑ size of each group

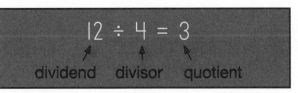

$12 \div 4 = 3$

dividend   divisor   quotient

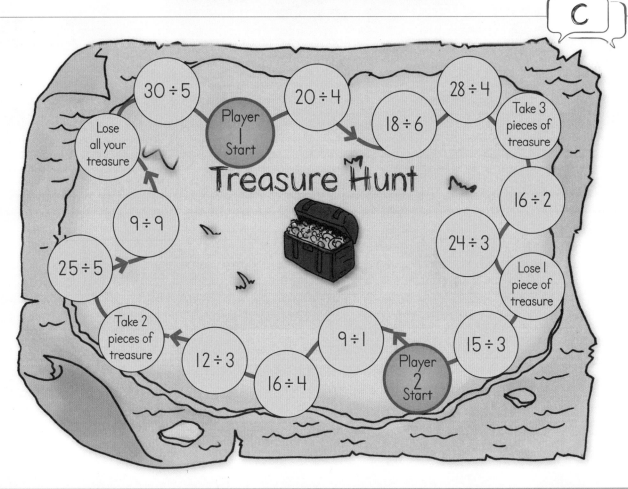

Practice 👤 Complete.

$20 \div 5$ = ▢ $90 \div 10$ = ▢ $16 \div 2$ = ▢

$30 \div 10$ = ▢ $25 \div 5$ = ▢ $15 \div 5$ = ▢

$10 \div 1$ = ▢ $20 \div 2$ = ▢ $50 \div 5$ = ▢

$45 \div 5$ = ▢ $40 \div 10$ = ▢ $14 \div 2$ = ▢

$18 \div 2$ = ▢ $35 \div 5$ = ▢ $70 \div 10$ = ▢

Color the problems that match the number in the star.

5

| $15 \div 3$ |
| $24 \div 4$ |
| $30 \div 6$ |

8

| $24 \div 3$ |
| $32 \div 4$ |
| $36 \div 6$ |

4

| $18 \div 3$ |
| $16 \div 4$ |
| $24 \div 6$ |

6

| $27 \div 3$ |
| $24 \div 4$ |
| $30 \div 5$ |

9

| $30 \div 3$ |
| $36 \div 4$ |
| $27 \div 3$ |

7

| $21 \div 3$ |
| $32 \div 4$ |
| $35 \div 5$ |

Review

Color the multiples in order from Start to End.

Multiples of 8

Start →

8	16	24	32	40
14	12	36	56	48
27	44	54	64	72
15	25	45	70	80
20	21	50	49	100

END

Multiples of 9

24	30	32	35	80
18	27	36	40	90
9	12	45	48	81
15	20	54	63	72
21	25	56	70	64

Start → **END**

Complete.

1 year = ☐ months

1 week = ☐ days

1 day = ☐ hours

1 hour = ☐ minutes

1 minute = ☐ seconds

Match pairs that equal 100.

79	33
67	42
58	55
45	21

Write the time.

1.4

Lesson Activities 👥

A

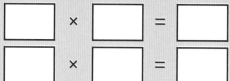

	×		=	

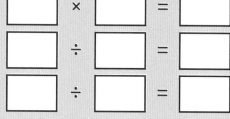

B

$35 \div 5 = \boxed{}$ $48 \div 6 = \boxed{}$

$5 \times \boxed{} = 35$ $6 \times \boxed{} = 48$

C

How to Read Word Problems

1. Read the problem.
2. Identify the goal.
3. Read the problem again.
   - Read slowly and carefully.
   - Imagine what's happening.
   - Stop after each sentence to make sure you understand it.
4. Solve.

Sammy is making bows from ribbon. She wants to make 5 bows. She needs 8 in. of ribbon for each bow. How much ribbon does she need?

Charlie is making bows from ribbon. He has 36 cm of ribbon. He wants to cut the ribbon into 4 equal parts. How long should he make each piece of ribbon?

Practice 👤 Complete.

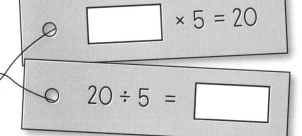
□ × 5 = 20
20 ÷ 5 = □

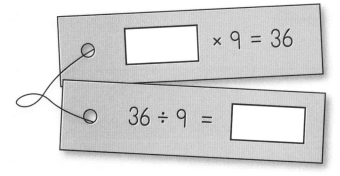
□ × 9 = 36
36 ÷ 9 = □

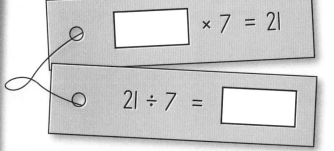
□ × 7 = 21
21 ÷ 7 = □

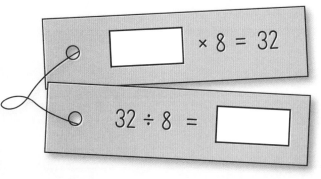
□ × 8 = 32
32 ÷ 8 = □

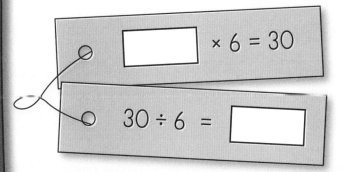
□ × 6 = 30
30 ÷ 6 = □

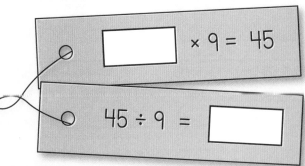
□ × 9 = 45
45 ÷ 9 = □

Solve. Write the equations you use.

The choir is setting up chairs for their concert. They have 36 chairs.
They put 9 chairs in each row.
How many rows can they make?

The actors are setting up chairs for their performance. They put 5 chairs in each row.
They make 6 rows.
How many chairs do they use?

Review 👤 Complete.

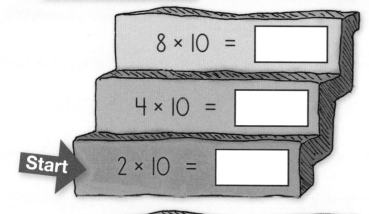

8 × 10 = [   ]

4 × 10 = [   ]

Start ▶ 2 × 10 = [   ]

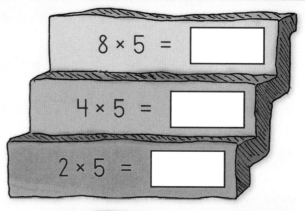

8 × 5 = [   ]

4 × 5 = [   ]

2 × 5 = [   ]

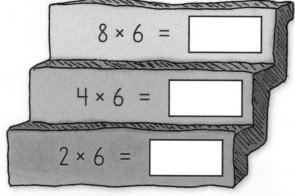

8 × 6 = [   ]

4 × 6 = [   ]

2 × 6 = [   ]

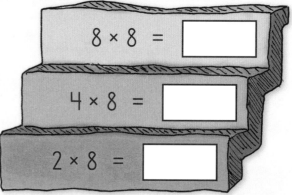

8 × 8 = [   ]

4 × 8 = [   ]

2 × 8 = [   ]

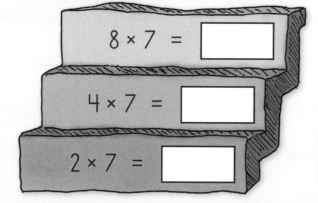

8 × 7 = [   ]

4 × 7 = [   ]

2 × 7 = [   ]

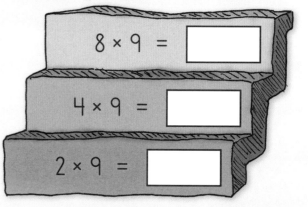

8 × 9 = [   ]

4 × 9 = [   ]

2 × 9 = [   ]

Choose the more sensible measurement for each item.

Height of a chair

| 1 centimeter | 1 meter |

Length of a ladybug

| 1 centimeter | 1 meter |

Length of a hike

| 1 meter | 1 kilometer |

Lesson Activities 👥

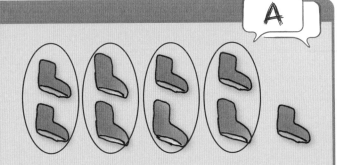

$8 ÷ 2 = 4$

8 can be evenly divided by 2.
8 is divisible by 2.

$9 ÷ 2 = 4 \, R1$

9 cannot be evenly divided by 2.
9 is not divisible by 2.

$12 ÷ 3 =$ ☐	$15 ÷ 3 =$ ☐	$16 ÷ 3 =$ ☐
$12 ÷ 4 =$ ☐	$15 ÷ 4 =$ ☐	$16 ÷ 4 =$ ☐
$12 ÷ 5 =$ ☐	$15 ÷ 5 =$ ☐	$16 ÷ 5 =$ ☐

B

Multiples of 2

2	4	6	8	10
12	14	16	18	20

Numbers divisible by 2 have

☐ in the ones-place.

Multiples of 5

5	10	15	20	25
30	35	40	45	50

Numbers divisible by 5 have

☐ in the ones-place.

Multiples of 10

10	20	30	40	50
60	70	80	90	100

Numbers divisible by 10 have

☐ in the ones-place.

Practice

Circle the numbers that match the description.
X the numbers that do not match the description.

Divisible by 2	Divisible by 10	Divisible by 5
(38) ~~41~~	70 68	37 80
96	90	35
790	500	100
205	130	95
324	704	453

Complete. Then, use the problems to answer the questions.

8 ÷ 3 = ☐   16 ÷ 4 = ☐   22 ÷ 6 = ☐

9 ÷ 3 = ☐   17 ÷ 4 = ☐   23 ÷ 6 = ☐

10 ÷ 3 = ☐   18 ÷ 4 = ☐   24 ÷ 6 = ☐

Is 8 divisible by 3?	Is 9 divisible by 3?
Is 16 divisible by 4?	Is 17 divisible by 4?
Is 18 divisible by 4?	Is 22 divisible by 6?
Is 23 divisible by 6?	Is 24 divisible by 6?

Review   Complete.

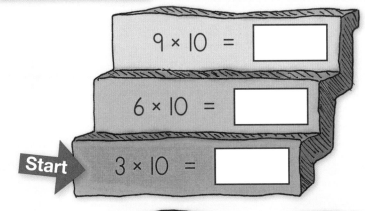

9 × 10 = ☐

6 × 10 = ☐

Start   3 × 10 = ☐

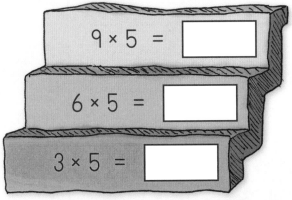

9 × 5 = ☐

6 × 5 = ☐

3 × 5 = ☐

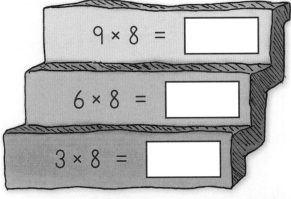

9 × 8 = ☐

6 × 8 = ☐

3 × 8 = ☐

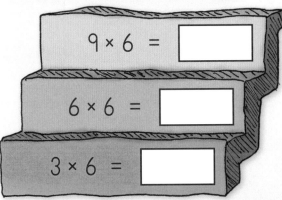

9 × 6 = ☐

6 × 6 = ☐

3 × 6 = ☐

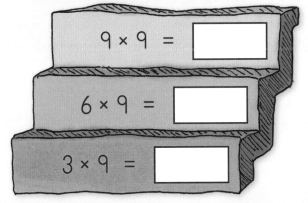

9 × 9 = ☐

6 × 9 = ☐

3 × 9 = ☐

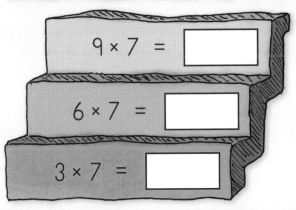

9 × 7 = ☐

6 × 7 = ☐

3 × 7 = ☐

Choose the more sensible measurement for each item.

Length of a paper clip

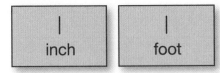

| 1 inch | 1 foot |

Length of a baseball bat

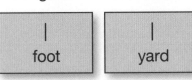

| 1 foot | 1 yard |

Width of a license plate

| 1 foot | 1 yard |

Lesson Activities 👥

A

The CHOCOLATE SHOP

Striped Chocolates

5 | 1 | 7

full boxes

chocolates in the full boxes

chocolates left

Caramel Chocolates

4 | 1 | 8

full boxes

chocolates in the full boxes

chocolates left

Cherry Chocolates

3 | 2 | 1

full boxes

chocolates in the full boxes

chocolates left

B

Long Division

1. Divide — How many groups can I make?

2. Multiply — How many are in the groups?

3. Subtract — How many are left?

4 | 1 | 4

1. Divide
2. Multiply
3. Subtract

2 | 1 | 5   5 | 2 | 6   3 | 1 | 1   4 | 3 | 7

Roll and Divide

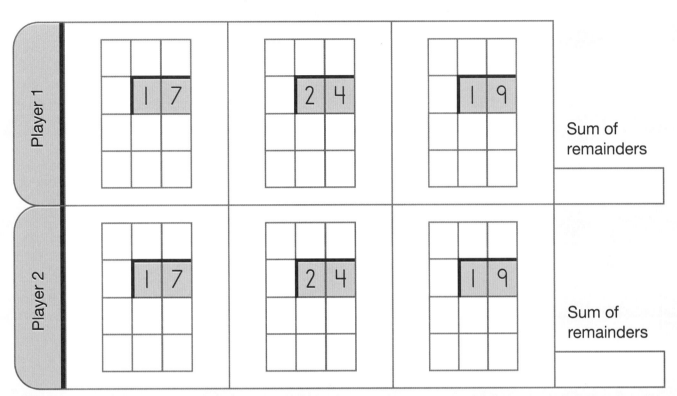

Player 1

| 1 | 7 | | 2 | 4 | | 1 | 9 |

Sum of remainders

Player 2

| 1 | 7 | | 2 | 4 | | 1 | 9 |

Sum of remainders

Practice 👤 Complete. Follow the steps.

1. Divide
2. Multiply
3. Subtract

5 | 1 8   5 | 2 3   9 | 3 2   4 | 2 6

Solve. Write the equations you use.

Oscar's mom runs 5 km every day. How many days does it take her to run 30 km?

Sophie's dad bikes 9 miles each day. How many days does it take for him to bike 45 miles?

Review

Choose the more sensible measurement for each item.

Slice of bread	Loaf of bread	Can of tomatoes

| 1 ounce | 1 pound | 1 ounce | 1 pound | 1 ounce | 1 pound |

Complete.

8:00 → 1 hr. → ☐

8:00 → 1 hr. 15 min. → ☐

8:00 → 1 hr. 30 min. → ☐

8:00 → 2 hr. → ☐

Complete.

	Double
30	60
40	
50	
12	
15	
17	

Circle the greatest number in each row.

7,014   7,040   7,004

8,296   8,298   8,030

6,405   6,350   6,399

Complete.

```
    3 8
 +  2 7
 ──────
```

```
    9 6
 +  4 5
 ──────
```

```
    8 7
 -  2 3
 ──────
```

```
    9 1
 -  4 8
 ──────
```

Lesson Activities 👥

Factor Pairs of 10	Factors of 10

$1 \times 10 \qquad 2 \times 5$ | $1 \quad 2 \quad 5 \quad 10$

Factor pairs of 20

$1 \times \boxed{}$

$2 \times \boxed{}$

$\boxed{} \times 5$

Factor pairs of 16

$1 \times \boxed{}$

$2 \times \boxed{}$

$\boxed{} \times 4$

Factor pairs of 11

$1 \times \boxed{}$

Factors Four in a Row

10	8	28	8	20
27	25	9	35	6
18	2	40	16	30
11	36	15	4	32
12	5	21	24	13

Practice

Complete the missing factors in the factor pairs.

Factor pairs of 6	Factor pairs of 7	Factor pairs of 9

$1 \times \boxed{}$

$2 \times \boxed{}$

$\boxed{} \times 7$

$1 \times \boxed{}$

$\boxed{} \times \boxed{}$

Factor pairs of 40	Factor pairs of 12	Factor pairs of 29

$\boxed{} \times 40$

2×20

$4 \times \boxed{}$

$5 \times \boxed{}$

$1 \times \boxed{}$

$2 \times \boxed{}$

$3 \times \boxed{}$

$\boxed{} \times \boxed{}$

Complete the factor triangles so each number in a box is the product of the factors in the adjoining circles.

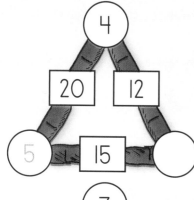

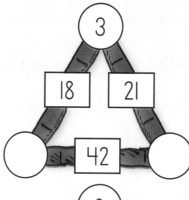

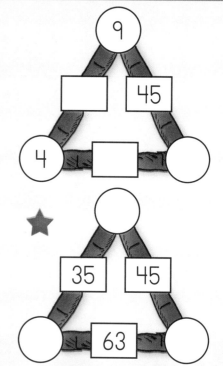

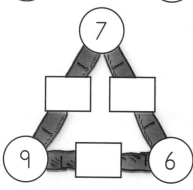

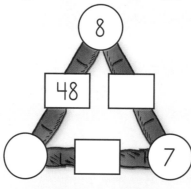

Review   👤   Complete. Follow the steps.

1. Divide
2. Multiply
3. Subtract

7 | 3 | 0   4 | 2 | 1   8 | 3 | 6   5 | 4 | 7

Match.

6 × 7	54	7 × 10	70
6 × 10	42	7 × 8	63
6 × 9	36	7 × 9	42
6 × 6	60	7 × 7	56
6 × 8	48	7 × 6	49

Color the shapes to match the fractions. Then, complete with <, >, or =.

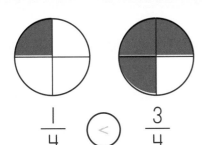

$$\frac{1}{4} \; < \; \frac{3}{4}$$

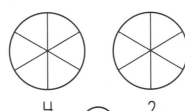

$$\frac{4}{6} \bigcirc \frac{2}{6}$$

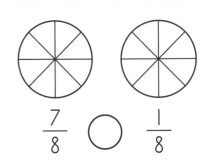

$$\frac{7}{8} \bigcirc \frac{1}{8}$$

Lesson Activities

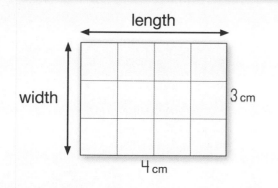

length

width

3 cm

4 cm

Perimeter of a Rectangle

length + width + length + width

Area of a Rectangle

length × width

B

Factor pairs of 12	Factor pairs of 16	Factor pairs of 9
Factor pairs of 6	Factor pairs of 8	Factor pairs of 10

C

 Roses 12 sq. ft.

 Sunflowers 16 sq. ft.

 Bluebells 9 sq. ft.

 Marigolds 6 sq. ft.

  Hostas 8 sq. ft.

 Lavender 10 sq. ft.

Player 1

Player 2

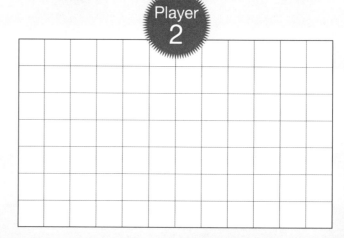

Practice 👤 Draw a rectangle with the given dimensions. Then, find the area and perimeter of the rectangle.

Length: 6 cm

Width: 4 cm

Perimeter: [　　　　] cm

Area: [　　　　] sq. cm

Length: 5 cm

Width: 5 cm

Perimeter: [　　　　] cm

Area: [　　　　] sq. cm

Find all factor pairs for each number. Then, draw a rectangle to match each factor pair.

Factor pairs of
18

Factor pairs of
20

Review

Choose the more sensible unit for each item.

Paper clip

I gram	I kilogram

Pineapple

I gram	I kilogram

Tack

I gram	I kilogram

Match.

8 × 8		72		9 × 9		54
8 × 9		48		9 × 6		90
8 × 7		64		9 × 10		63
8 × 6		80		9 × 7		72
8 × 10		56		9 × 8		81

Complete.

3 weeks = ☐ days

3 weeks, 5 days = ☐ days

28 days = ☐ weeks

30 days = ☐ weeks, ☐ days

24

Lesson 1.8

Lesson Activities 👥

Factor pairs of 24		
1	2	3
4	5	6
7	8	9

A

Factor pairs of 30		
1	2	3
4	5	6
7	8	9

B

Factor Blast

2	16	3	28	4	8
5	14	6	23	7	21	8	27
9	15	10	17	11	12	12	25

Number	Factor Pairs	Sum of Factors
Player 1 Total		

Number	Factor Pairs	Sum of Factors
Player 2 Total		

Practice

Find all factor pairs for each number.

Factor pairs of
14

1	2	3
4	5	6
7	8	9

Factor pairs of
28

1	2	3
4	5	6
7	8	9

Factor pairs of
15

1	2	3
4	5	6
7	8	9

Factor pairs of
35

1	2	3
4	5	6
7	8	9

Factor pairs of
23

1	2	3
4	5	6
7	8	9

Factor pairs of
27

1	2	3
4	5	6
7	8	9

Factor pairs of
32

1	2	3
4	5	6
7	8	9

★

Factor pairs of
36

1	2	3
4	5	6
7	8	9

Review 👤 Find the perimeter and area of each shape.

7 cm

2 cm

Perimeter: ⬜ cm

Area: ⬜ sq. cm

6 cm

3 cm

Perimeter: ⬜ cm

Area: ⬜ sq. cm

Complete.

×	6	7	8	9	10
5					
6					
7					
8					
9					

Complete.

⬜ ⬅ 1 hr. | 10:30

⬜ ⬅ 1 hr. 15 min. | 10:30

⬜ ⬅ 1 hr. 30 min. | 10:30

⬜ ⬅ 2 hr. | 10:30

Solve. Write the equations you use.

There are 6 groups of children at day camp. There are 8 children in each group. How many children are at day camp?

There are 45 children at gymnastics lessons. The teachers divide the children into 5 equal groups. How many children are in each group?

Lesson Activities 👥

Prime numbers have exactly 2 factors: 1 and the number itself.

2	5	19
1 × 2	1 × 5	1 × 19

Composite numbers have more than 2 factors.

4	12	21
1 × 4	1 × 12	1 × 21
2 × 2	2 × 6	3 × 7
	3 × 4	

1	2	3	4	5	6	7	8	9	10
11	12	13	14	15	16	17	18	19	20

Number Knock-Out

Player 1

40   47   44   43
37   30   23   25
21   49   27   42
38   29   35   31

Player 2

40   47   44   43
37   30   23   25
21   49   27   42
38   29   35   31

Practice

Find all factor pairs for each number.

Factor pairs of 18

1	2	3
4	5	6
7	8	9

Factor pairs of 31

1	2	3
4	5	6
7	8	9

Factor pairs of 12

1	2	3
4	5	6
7	8	9

Factor pairs of 50

1	2	3
4	5	6
7	8	9

Is 18 prime or composite?

Is 31 prime or composite?

Is 12 prime or composite?

Is 50 prime or composite?

List the factors of 18 in order from least to greatest.

List the factors of 50 in order from least to greatest.

Is 4 a factor of 12?

Is 4 a factor of 50?

Review   Circle the description that matches the angle.

Right angle	Right angle	Right angle
Smaller than a right angle	Smaller than a right angle	Smaller than a right angle
Larger than a right angle	Larger than a right angle	Larger than a right angle

Complete.

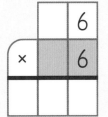

1. Divide
2. Multiply
3. Subtract

8 ⌐2 5⌐   2 ⌐1 7⌐   6 ⌐4 0⌐   7 ⌐6 8⌐

Complete.

| | 6 | | | 8 | | | 9 | | | 8 | | | 3 |
| × | 6 | × | 9 | × | 6 | × | 8 | × | 7 |

| | 8 | | | 7 | | | 7 | | | 5 | | | 9 |
| × | 6 | × | 7 | × | 8 | × | 7 | × | 9 |

| | 9 | | | 8 | | | 7 | | | 9 | | | 6 |
| × | 5 | × | 9 | × | 4 | × | 7 | × | 7 |

Unit Wrap-Up

Circle the numbers that match the description.
X the numbers that do not match the description.

Multiples of 4	Multiples of 7	Multiples of 5
12 1 8	27 7 17	15 12 20
2 4 20	14 70 35	49 35 25

Factors of 16	Factors of 7	Factors of 9
16 4 1	2 7 3	6 18 1
14 2 8	1 17 14	9 3 15

Divisible by 2	Divisible by 10	Divisible by 5
8 54 81	80 20 45	25 35 100
49 36 27	406 400 650	215 50 95

Find all factor pairs for each number.

Factor pairs of 12		Factor pairs of 40	
	1 2 3		1 2 3
	4 5 6		4 5 6
	7 8 9		7 8 9

Unit Wrap-Up

Circle the prime numbers.
X the composite numbers.

| 7 | 13 | 9 | 11 | 25 |

| 18 | 2 | 5 | 14 | 23 |

Use these numbers to answer the riddles. You will not use every number.

| 10 | 15 | 17 | 20 | 25 | 27 | 29 | 36 | 42 |

This number is greater than 17. It is a multiple of 5. It is divisible by 2.	This number is greater than 17. It is a multiple of 5. It is not divisible by 2.
This number is less than 20. It is a multiple of 3.	This number is less than 20. It is prime.
This number has 1, 3, 9, and 27 as its factors.	This number is greater than 20. It is prime.
This number is a multiple of 6. It is also a multiple of 7.	This number is a multiple of 9. It has 4 as one of its factors.

Lesson Activities 👥

Larry's Used Vehicles — Big Sale!

Golf Cart $3,217   All-terrain Vehicle $4,605   Motorcycle $6,991

A

| | thousands | hundreds | tens | ones |

Standard Form	Expanded Form
3,217	3,000 + 200 + 10 + 7
4,605	
6,991	

B

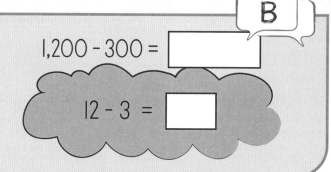

600 + 800 = ☐

6 + 8 = ☐

1,200 − 300 = ☐

12 − 3 = ☐

C

Close to 3,000

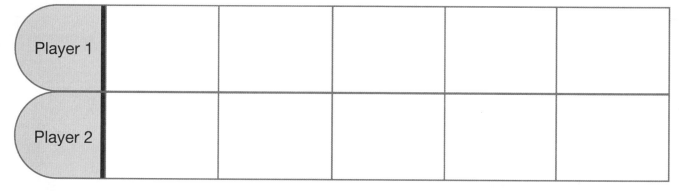

Player 1					
Player 2					

Practice

Complete the missing numbers.

$$8{,}974 = 8{,}000 + 900 + 70 + \boxed{}$$

$$1{,}293 = 1{,}000 + \boxed{} + 90 + 3$$

$$3{,}040 = 3{,}000 + \boxed{}$$

$$\boxed{} = 5{,}000 + 7$$

Match.

1,300 + 600	1,700	2,200 - 300
1,700 + 300	1,900	2,400 - 400
1,900 + 600	2,000	2,000 - 300
800 + 900	2,200	3,100 - 600
1,400 + 800	2,500	3,000 - 800

Connect each number to its dot on the number line.

| 2,350 | 235 | 4,700 | 5,625 | 8,777 |

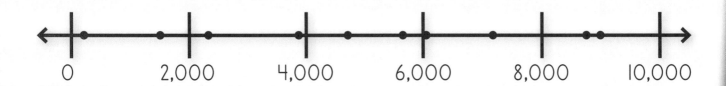

| 3,879 | 1,500 | 6,025 | 9,000 | 7,116 |

Review

Color the problems that match the number in the star.

5

35 ÷ 7
32 ÷ 8
45 ÷ 9

4

45 ÷ 9
28 ÷ 7
32 ÷ 8

2

16 ÷ 8
27 ÷ 9
14 ÷ 7

3

24 ÷ 8
28 ÷ 7
27 ÷ 9

Complete with <, >, or =.

4,302 ◯ 4,032

6,710 ◯ 6,701

8,056 ◯ 8,560

9,790 ◯ 979

1,099 ◯ 1,990

Complete.

2:40 → 15 min. → [ ]

2:45 → 15 min. → [ ]

2:50 → 15 min. → [ ]

2:55 → 15 min. → [ ]

3:00 → 15 min. → [ ]

Use the clues to complete the chart.

- Sadie is 20 cm shorter than Cayden.

- Sadie is 6 cm taller than Ben.

- Sadie is 8 cm shorter than Leena.

Name	Height (cm)
Cayden	145
Sadie	
Ben	
Leena	

Lesson Activities 👥

Nearest Hundred

$$\longleftarrow \quad | \qquad | \qquad | \quad \longrightarrow$$
200   300

$2\underline{7}4 \approx$ ☐

Nearest Ten

$$\longleftarrow \quad | \qquad | \qquad | \quad \longrightarrow$$
270   280

$27\underline{4} \approx$ ☐

☐   ☐

$\underline{4}45 \approx$ ☐

☐   ☐

$4\underline{4}5 \approx$ ☐

☐   ☐

$\underline{8}96 \approx$ ☐

☐   ☐

$8\underline{9}6 \approx$ ☐

Rounding Four in a Row

570	$\underline{8}49$	210	$5\underline{7}1$	300	$\underline{4}25$
$2\underline{9}6$	400	$\underline{9}32$	900	$3\underline{9}8$	800
300	$21\underline{4}$	570	$\underline{7}50$	400	$2\underline{6}1$
$\underline{2}07$	800	$\underline{8}83$	210	$5\underline{6}5$	900

Practice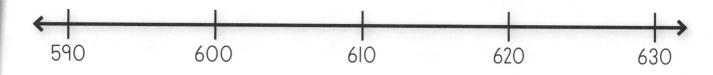

**Round each number to the nearest ten.
Use the number line to help.**

←——|————————|————————|————————|————————|——→
590   600   610   620   630

6|2 ≈ [ ]   6_0_4 ≈ [ ]

6_2_5 ≈ [ ]   591 ≈ [ ]

59_6_ ≈ [ ]   6|9 ≈ [ ]

Round each number to the underlined place.

_8_74 ≈ [ ]   9|9 ≈ [ ]

_3_09 ≈ [ ]   73_5_ ≈ [ ]

_5_62 ≈ [ ]   4_0_4 ≈ [ ]

_6_50 ≈ [ ]   69_8_ ≈ [ ]

Round each price to the underlined place.

 $797

_4_38 ≈ [ ]   _7_97 ≈ [ ]   _9_64 ≈ [ ]

43_8_ ≈ [ ]   79_7_ ≈ [ ]   96_4_ ≈ [ ]

Review   Complete.

[ ]	← 20 min.	4:30
[ ]	← 20 min.	4:20
[ ]	← 20 min.	4:10
[ ]	← 20 min.	4:00

Complete.

```
    3 9 7
  +　2 0 6
  _____
```

```
    4 2 8
  +　7 9 0
  _____
```

```
    6 4 8
  -　1 7 3
  _____
```

```
    7 0 7
  -　2 4 5
  _____
```

Use the chart to answer the questions. Write the equations you use.

How much does skating cost for 4 guests?

ROLLER SKATING BIRTHDAY PARTY OPTIONS

Skating.............. $7
Skate rental........ $3
Party favors........ $4

All prices are per guest.

How much does skating cost for 8 guests?

How much does skating and skate rental cost for 5 guests?

How much does skating and skate rental cost for 10 guests?

How much does skating, skate rental, and party favors cost for 10 guests?

 How much does skating, skate rental, and party favors cost for 11 guests?

Lesson Activities 👥

Nearest Thousand

5,371 ≈ [   ]   [   ]   [   ]

←———|———————|———————|———→

Nearest Hundred

5,371 ≈ [   ]   [   ]   [   ]

←——|———————|———————|——→

Nearest Ten

5,371 ≈ [   ]   [   ]   [   ]

←——|———————|———————|——→

4,628 ≈ [ ]	8,409 ≈ [ ]	6,965 ≈ [ ]
4,628 ≈ [ ]	8,409 ≈ [ ]	6,965 ≈ [ ]
4,628 ≈ [ ]	8,409 ≈ [ ]	6,965 ≈ [ ]

Dice Tic-Tac Toe

9,172	7,262	2,508	6,454	5,885
1,617	4,210	7,379	3,463	2,193
3,726	5,995	8,789	6,850	4,344
5,001	6,638	9,517	1,036	8,942

Practice

Round each number to the nearest ten.
Use the number line to help.

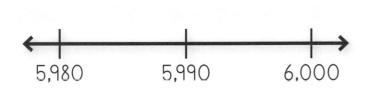

5,980   5,990   6,000

5,9<u>9</u>2 ≈ [ ]

5,9<u>9</u>7 ≈ [ ]

5,9<u>8</u>5 ≈ [ ]

Round each number to the underlined place.

<u>5</u>,062 ≈ [ ]   3,9<u>9</u>9 ≈ [ ]

6,<u>0</u>49 ≈ [ ]   2,<u>9</u>95 ≈ [ ]

1,0<u>0</u>7 ≈ [ ]   4,9<u>9</u>1 ≈ [ ]

8,0<u>0</u>3 ≈ [ ]   7,<u>9</u>93 ≈ [ ]

Round each number to the underlined place.

Weight of a hippopotamus:

2,864 kilograms

<u>2</u>,864 ≈ [ ]

2,<u>8</u>64 ≈ [ ]

2,8<u>6</u>4 ≈ [ ]

Distance from Los Angeles
to New York City:

4,473 kilometers

<u>4</u>,473 ≈ [ ]

4,<u>4</u>73 ≈ [ ]

4,4<u>7</u>3 ≈ [ ]

Review

Match.

70 ÷ 7	6	48 ÷ 6
42 ÷ 7	7	36 ÷ 6
63 ÷ 7	8	60 ÷ 6
49 ÷ 7	9	42 ÷ 6
56 ÷ 7	10	54 ÷ 6

Find the perimeter and area.

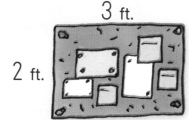

3 ft.

2 ft.

Perimeter: _____ ft.

Area: _____ sq. ft.

2 km

1 km

Perimeter: _____ km

Area: _____ sq. km

5 in.

8 in.

Perimeter: _____ in.

Area: _____ sq. in.

Circle the prime numbers.

(2)	(3)	4
5	6	7
8	9	10
11	12	13
14	15	16
17	18	19

Complete.

$100 = 90 +$ _____

_____ $= 250 + 250$

$400 =$ _____ $+ 300$

_____ $= 300 - 50$

$150 = 250 -$ _____

$100 =$ _____ $- 50$

Lesson Activities 👥

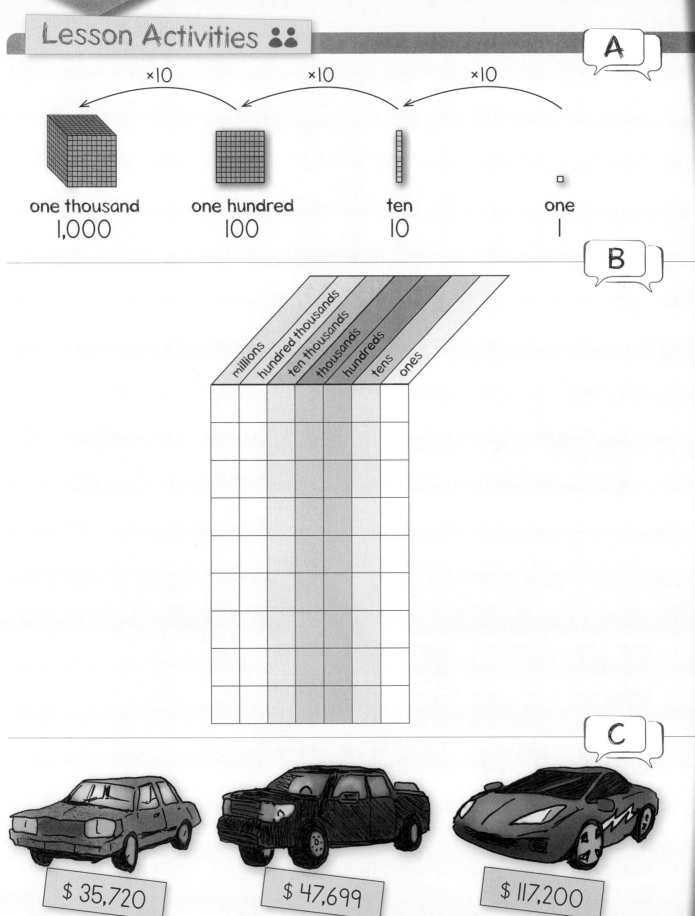

×10   ×10   ×10

one thousand   one hundred   ten   one
1,000   100   10   1

B

millions	hundred thousands	ten thousands	thousands	hundreds	tens	ones

C

$ 35,720 $ 47,699 $ 117,200

Practice

Write each number in the place-value chart.

	millions	hundred thousands	ten thousands	thousands	hundreds	tens	ones
six thousand							
nine hundred							
five hundred thousand							
ten thousand							
twenty thousand							
eighty thousand							
four million							
three hundred thousand							
seven							

Match.

200,907	twenty-nine thousand seven hundred
29,700	twenty thousand nine hundred seven
209,070	two hundred thousand nine hundred seven
20,907	two hundred nine thousand seventy

Review

Complete the mixed-up multiplication chart.

×	2	4	10	9	1	3	5	6	8	7
5	10	20	50	45	5	15	25	30	40	35
6			60		6		30			
7	14		70		7					

Complete.

```
  3,9 4 2
+ 4,3 0 8
_____

```

```
  6,9 8 1
- 4,6 3 5
_____

```

```
  3,2 2 4
- 1,3 8 6
_____

```

Choose the more sensible unit for each item.

Capacity of a tea cup

 | cup
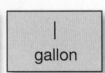 | gallon

Capacity of a watering can

| cup
| gallon

Capacity of a pitcher

| cup
| gallon

Answer the questions.

Is 45 a multiple of 5?	Is 32 a multiple of 6?
Is 27 divisible by 2?	Is 40 divisible by 10?
Is 4 a factor of 18?	Is 6 a factor of 24?

Lesson Activities

A

millions	hundred thousands	ten thousands	thousands	hundreds	tens	ones	
		4	6,2	0	5	→	
			2	0,3	8	6	→
	4	0	7,0	3	1	→	
1,	0	6	0,4	2	7	→	

B

sailboat

$

airboat

$

speed boat

$

yacht

$

pontoon boat

$

cabin cruiser

$

Practice 👤 Complete.

Standard Form	Expanded Form
24,923	
35,607	
	50,000 + 4,000 + 900 + 80 + 5
120,082	
	500,000 + 40,000 + 10 + 9

Complete with <, >, or =.

96,000 ◯ 97,000   36,845 ◯ 51,936   401,560 ◯ 401,506

85,422 ◯ 85,088   77,201 ◯ 77,201   635,785 ◯ 695,014

19,874 ◯ 20,000   46,500 ◯ 45,600   999,999 ◯ 999,998

Circle the greatest number in each group.

37,405	543,000	197,452
36,943	529,999	197,099
38,000	500,682	197,800

Review 👤 Complete. Follow the steps.

1. Divide
2. Multiply
3. Subtract

5 | 1 | 9   5 | 2 | 9   5 | 3 | 9   5 | 4 | 9

Match pairs that equal 10,000.

9,000   2,000

8,500   3,000

8,000   1,000

7,500   2,500

7,000   1,500

Complete.

8:00	20	min. ➡	8:20
8:20		min. ➡	8:40
8:40		min. ➡	8:55
8:55		min. ➡	9:00
9:00		min. ➡	9:25

Solve. Write the equations you use.

The remote-controlled car costs $59.
The remote-controlled helicopter costs
$33 more than the car.
How much does it cost to buy both?

Jonah has $35.
He wants to buy a video game
controller that costs $54.
How much more money
does he need?

A

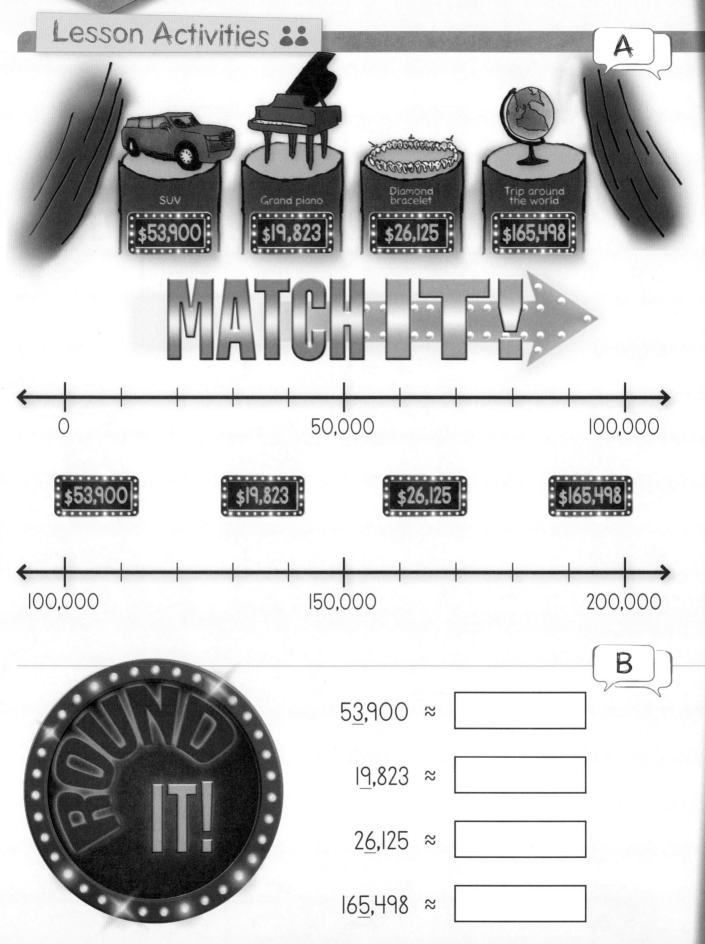

SUV
$53,900

Grand piano
$19,823

Diamond bracelet
$26,125

Trip around the world
$165,498

MATCH IT!

$53,900 $19,823 $26,125 $165,498

0   50,000   100,000

100,000   150,000   200,000

B

ROUND IT!

53,900 ≈ [   ]

19,823 ≈ [   ]

26,125 ≈ [   ]

165,498 ≈ [   ]

Practice

Round each number to the nearest thousand. Use the number line to help.

←――――|――――|――――|――――|――――|→
58,000   59,000   60,000   61,000   62,000

60,389 ≈ [   ]   58,499 ≈ [   ]

61,700 ≈ [   ]   59,825 ≈ [   ]

59,074 ≈ [   ]   61,009 ≈ [   ]

←――――|――――|――――|――――|――――|→
748,000   749,000   750,000   751,000   752,000

751,132 ≈ [   ]   750,500 ≈ [   ]

748,510 ≈ [   ]   749,999 ≈ [   ]

751,647 ≈ [   ]   751,008 ≈ [   ]

Round each number to the nearest thousand to complete the chart.

Zoo Attendance

Month	Attendance	Rounded to Nearest Thousand
May	225,882	
June	358,947	
July	429,694	
August	344,006	

Review

Find all factor pairs. | **Complete.**

Factor pairs of
18

```
1   2   3
4   5   6
7   8   9
```

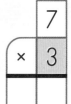
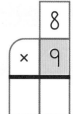

Factor pairs of
24

```
1   2   3
4   5   6
7   8   9
```

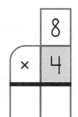

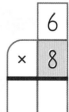

Circle the shapes that have 4 right angles.
X the shapes that do not have 4 right angles.

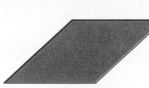
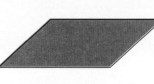

Complete.

6 weeks = [ ] days   28 days = [ ] weeks

6 weeks, 1 day = [ ] days   29 days = [ ] weeks, [ ] day(s)

9 weeks = [ ] days   49 days = [ ] weeks

9 weeks, 5 days = [ ] days   50 days = [ ] weeks, [ ] day(s)

Lesson Activities

A

35,000 + 5,000 = ☐

35 + 5 = ☐

142,000 + 100,000 = ☐

142 + 100 = ☐

90,000 - 30,000 = ☐

90 - 30 = ☐

200,000 - 50,000 = ☐

200 - 50 = ☐

B

 = 5,000

= 10,000

= 15,000

= 20,000

= 25,000

= 30,000

0, 1, or 2 of a Kind = 0

4 of a Kind = 50,000

5 of a Kind = 100,000

6 of a Kind = 150,000

Race to 500,000

Player 1	Player 2

2.7

Practice

Match pairs that equal 100,000.

| 50,000 | | 25,000 |

| 99,000 | | 10,000 |

| 75,000 | | 50,000 |

| 90,000 | | 15,000 |

| 85,000 | | 1,000 |

Complete.

$60,000 + 50,000 = \boxed{}$	$100,000 + 200,000 = \boxed{}$
$80,000 - 10,000 = \boxed{}$	$300,000 + 50,000 = \boxed{}$
$45,000 + 5,000 = \boxed{}$	$300,000 - 50,000 = \boxed{}$
$50,000 - 25,000 = \boxed{}$	$400,000 - 100,000 = \boxed{}$

Solve. Write the equations you use.

Peter bikes 20,000 meters on Monday and 13,000 meters on Tuesday.
How much further does he bike on Monday than Tuesday?

Vanshika's mom runs 6,000 meters on Saturday and 8,000 meters on Sunday.
How far does she run in all?

Review

Match.

90 ÷ 9	6	72 ÷ 8
72 ÷ 9	7	56 ÷ 8
54 ÷ 9	8	48 ÷ 8
81 ÷ 9	9	80 ÷ 8
63 ÷ 9	10	64 ÷ 8

Match.

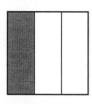

$\frac{1}{3}$

$\frac{1}{6}$

$\frac{1}{8}$

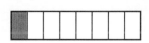
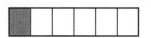

Solve. Write the equations you use.

On Saturday, the ice cream shop sold 125 ice cream cones. 50 were chocolate. 35 were vanilla. The rest were strawberry. How many were strawberry?

Bobby's family bought 4 chocolate cones and 3 strawberry cones. Each cone cost $6. How much did they pay for all the ice cream cones?

Lesson Activities 👥

	2	4	9	,	3	1	2
+	1	0	6	,	8	4	8

	6	5	7	,	9	0	8
−	2	6	1	,	3	5	4

Leaf Fight

Player 1	Player 2

467,890

128,365

38,704

333,333

99,999

209,999

56,001

8,998

519,786

19,643

Practice 👤 Complete.

	5	3	9	,	0	8	7
+	2	4	6	,	3	5	3

	5	3	9	,	0	8	7
−	2	4	6	,	3	5	3

Review 👤 Choose the more sensible unit for each item.

Capacity of an eyedropper

I mL	I L

Capacity of a water bottle

I mL	I L

Capacity of a pitcher

I mL	I L

Round to the underlined place.

7$\underline{3}$8 ≈ ☐

4,3$\underline{6}$2 ≈ ☐

8,$\underline{9}$74 ≈ ☐

3$\underline{6}$,527 ≈ ☐

8$\underline{4}$,014 ≈ ☐

Complete.

3 × 8 = ☐   9 × 7 = ☐

7 × 7 = ☐   4 × 9 = ☐

8 × 9 = ☐   8 × 7 = ☐

9 × 3 = ☐   4 × 7 = ☐

7 × 6 = ☐   9 × 9 = ☐

Lesson Activities 👥

37,406 people came to the baseball game on Thursday.
48,694 people came to the baseball game on Friday.
What was the total attendance for both games?

➡️ How many more people came to the baseball game on Friday than the game on Thursday?

The aquarium sold 137,892 child tickets in October.
It sold 45,624 fewer adult tickets than child tickets.
How many adult tickets did the aquarium sell?

➡️ How many child and adult tickets did the aquarium sell in all?

Practice

**Use the chart to answer the questions.
Write the equations you use.**

State	Population in 1900	Population in 2000
North Dakota	319,146	642,200
South Dakota	401,570	754,844

How many people lived in North Dakota and South Dakota in 1900?

How many more people lived in South Dakota than North Dakota in 2000?

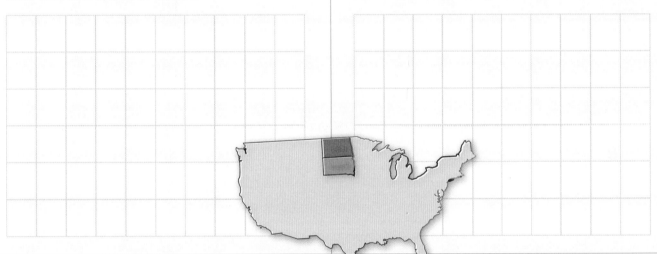

How much did North Dakota's population grow from 1900 to 2000?

How much did South Dakota's population grow from 1900 to 2000?

2.9

Review 👤 Color the problems that match the number in the star.

 7

49 ÷ 7
56 ÷ 8
90 ÷ 9
28 ÷ 4

 6

54 ÷ 9
56 ÷ 7
48 ÷ 8
30 ÷ 5

 9

72 ÷ 8
81 ÷ 9
56 ÷ 7
36 ÷ 4

 8

72 ÷ 8
56 ÷ 7
72 ÷ 9
24 ÷ 3

Tell how many right angles each shape has.

☐ right angle(s)

☐ right angle(s)

☐ right angle(s)

Match.

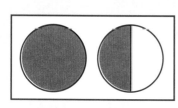

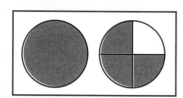

 $1\frac{1}{4}$

 $1\frac{3}{8}$

$1\frac{1}{2}$

$1\frac{3}{4}$

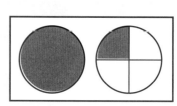

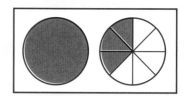

Unit Wrap-Up 👤 Write each number in standard form.

Words	Standard Form
five hundred thousand six hundred twenty	
five hundred six thousand twenty	
fifty-six thousand two hundred	
fifty-six thousand two	
five hundred sixty-two thousand	

Write each number in expanded form.

75,978 =

395,100 =

130,891 =

Round to the underlined place.

3,7̲82 ≈

4,9̲61 ≈

5,9̲85 ≈

3̲6,847 ≈

65̲9,285 ≈

Use the clues to solve the number riddle.

- I am greater than 80,000 and less than 81,000.

- The digit in my tens-place is 3.

- The digit in my hundreds-place is 2 more than the digit in my tens-place.

- I am divisible by 10.

☐☐,☐☐☐

Unit Wrap-Up

Complete.

300,000 + 100,000 = ☐

300,000 + 37,000 = ☐

99,000 + 3,000 = ☐

100,000 - 35,000 = ☐

100,000 - 1,000 = ☐

150,000 - 25,000 = ☐

Complete with <, >, or =.

99,999 ◯ 100,000

74,017 ◯ 74,701

513,284 ◯ 531,284

680,562 ◯ 680,000

739,865 ◯ 739,864

297,842 ◯ 297,842

Complete.

	5	9	7	,	3	4	6
+	1	0	2	,	6	5	4

	6	7	4	,	0	3	9
−	2	9	1	,	5	2	8

	2	9	9	,	9	9	9
+	3	7	5	,	8	6	4

	5	7	5	,	1	7	5
−	1	6	2	,	3	8	5

Solve. Write the equations you use.

The bookstore had $474,968 in sales this year. It had $439,470 in sales last year. What were its total sales for both years?

→ How much greater were the bookstore's sales this year than last year?

Lesson Activities 👥

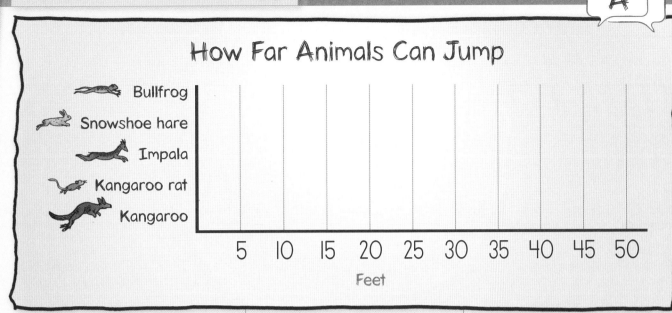

How Far Animals Can Jump

A bullfrog can jump 6 ft. A snowshoe hare can jump 2 times as far as a bullfrog. How far can a showshoe hare jump?

➡ How many feet farther can a snowshoe hare jump than a bullfrog?

An impala can jump 5 times as far as a bullfrog. How far can an impala jump?

➡ How many feet less can a bullfrog jump than an impala?

A kangaroo can jump 45 ft. That's 5 times as far as a kangaroo rat can jump. How far can a kangaroo rat jump?

➡ How many feet farther can a kangaroo jump than a kangaroo rat?

World record for broad jump:

12 ft.

My broad jump distance:

☐ ft.

The world record is _____ feet longer than my jump.

The world record is _____ times as long as my jump.

Practice

Betsy asked people what their favorite season is. Use the clues to complete her bar graph.

- 6 people chose spring.

- 2 fewer people chose summer than spring.

- Twice as many people chose fall as summer.

- 4 times as many people chose fall as winter.

Use the clues to complete the chart.

- Peter is 2 years older than Nora.

- Hannah is twice as old as Nora.

- Mom is 6 times as old as Peter.

- Dad is 5 times as old as Hannah.

Name	Age
Nora	4
Peter	
Hannah	
Mom	
Dad	

Use the clues to complete the prices.

- The pogo stick costs 6 times as much as the jump rope.

- The skateboard costs $2 less than the pogo stick.

- The mini trampoline costs twice as much as the skateboard.

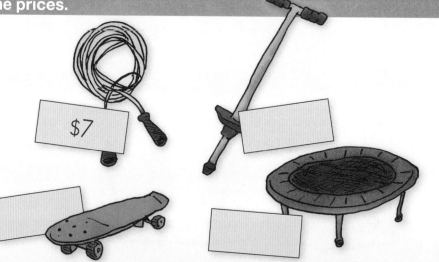

Review

Complete. Follow the steps.

1. Divide

2. Multiply

3. Subtract

| | 4 | 3 6 | | 5 | 3 6 | | 6 | 3 6 | | 7 | 3 6 |

4 ⟌ 3 6   5 ⟌ 3 6   6 ⟌ 3 6   7 ⟌ 3 6

Write the quantities in the place-value chart. | **Complete.**

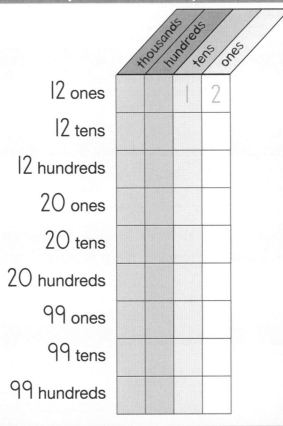

	thousands	hundreds	tens	ones
12 ones			1	2
12 tens				
12 hundreds				
20 ones				
20 tens				
20 hundreds				
99 ones				
99 tens				
99 hundreds				

	5	4,	3	9	2
+	8	7,	1	0	6

	9	7,	3	0	4
−	4	5,	6	1	7

Solve the number riddles.

The product of two numbers is 12.
The sum of the numbers is 7.
What are the two numbers?

The product of two numbers is 40.
The difference between the numbers is 3.
What are the two numbers?

The product of two numbers is 19.
The sum of the numbers is 20.
What are the two numbers?

 The product of two numbers is 100.
The sum of the numbers is 25.
What are the two numbers?

3.2

Lesson Activities 👥

A

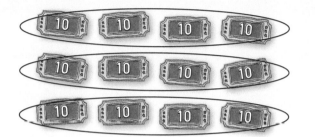

$3 \times 40 = \boxed{}$

3×4 tens $= \boxed{}$ tens

$4 \times 500 = \boxed{}$

4×5 hundreds $= \boxed{}$ hundreds

$2 \times 8,000 = \boxed{}$

2×8 thousands $= \boxed{}$ thousands

B

1. Underline the place-holder zeros.

2. Multiply the non-zero digits.

3. Tack on the place-holder zeros.

$4 \times 60 = \boxed{}$

$3 \times 700 = \boxed{}$

$5 \times 2,000 = \boxed{}$

$2 \times 90 = \boxed{}$

$5 \times 3,000 = \boxed{}$

$8 \times 500 = \boxed{}$

$8 \times 4,000 = \boxed{}$

$4 \times 400 = \boxed{}$

$5 \times 60 = \boxed{}$

MENTAL MATH ARCADE

PRIZES

☐	×	80				
☐	×	500				
☐	×	700				
☐	×	2,000				
☐	×	3,000				

Total Points

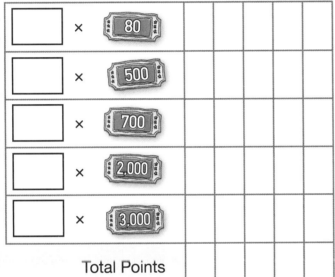

6,000

8,000

15,000

20,000

Practice

Complete.

2 × 7,000 = ☐   5 × 600 = ☐

9 × 40 = ☐   3 × 8,000 = ☐

6 × 800 = ☐   4 × 70 = ☐

7 × 500 = ☐   9 × 9,000 = ☐

★ ☐ × 6,000 = 36,000   ★ 8 × ☐ = 40,000

Review

Circle the numbers that match the description.
X the numbers that do not match the description.

Divisible by 2		Divisible by 5		Divisible by 10	
3,295	7,438	3,295	7,438	3,295	7,438
2,100	5,335	2,100	5,335	2,100	5,335
1,926	8,750	1,926	8,750	1,926	8,750

Complete with <, >, or =.

694,228 ◯ 64,228

135,017 ◯ 301,000

42,986 ◯ 429,861

543,908 ◯ 543,908

76,209 ◯ 76,290

Match.

$\frac{2}{3}$
$\frac{2}{6}$
$\frac{2}{2}$
$\frac{2}{4}$

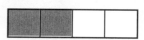

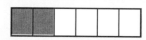

Solve. Write the equations you use.

Sean's parents pay $2,694 for new carpet.
They pay $3,047 for new furniture.
How much do they spend in all?

 How much more does the furniture cost than the carpet?

Lesson Activities 👥

A

$3 \times 900 =$ ☐ $4 \times 4{,}000 =$ ☐

B

$20 \times 30 =$ ☐

2 tens × 3 tens = ☐ hundreds

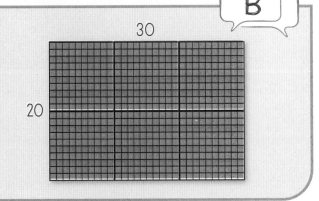

30

20

$40 \times 40 =$ ☐ $60 \times 30 =$ ☐ $80 \times 50 =$ ☐

C

SPIN TO WIN!

			Product
☐	×	☐	☐
☐	×	☐	☐
☐	×	☐	☐
☐	×	☐	☐

Player 1 Total ☐

			Product
☐	×	☐	☐
☐	×	☐	☐
☐	×	☐	☐
☐	×	☐	☐

Player 2 Total ☐

Practice 👤 Complete.

$30 \times 30 = $ ☐ $20 \times 90 = $ ☐

$10 \times 70 = $ ☐ $60 \times 50 = $ ☐

$7 \times 70 = $ ☐ $90 \times 90 = $ ☐

$60 \times 60 = $ ☐ $6 \times 800 = $ ☐

$80 \times 70 = $ ☐ $70 \times 60 = $ ☐

$8 \times 9,000 = $ ☐ $40 \times 90 = $ ☐

Solve. Write the equations you use.

There are 50 paper clips in each box.
How many paper clips are in 20 boxes?

Logan earns $30 per hour.
He works 40 hours per week.
How much does he earn in one week?

There are 60 seconds in each minute.
How many seconds are in 30 minutes?

There are 60 seconds in each minute.
How many seconds are in 60 minutes?

Review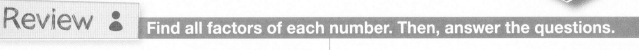

Find all factors of each number. Then, answer the questions.

Factor pairs of 19	1 2 3 4 5 6 7 8 9

Is 19 prime or composite?

Is 19 a multiple of 4?

Is 5 a factor of 19?

Factor pairs of 20	1 2 3 4 5 6 7 8 9

Is 20 prime or composite?

Is 20 a multiple of 4?

Is 5 a factor of 20?

Round to the underlined place.	**Match pairs that equal 10,000.**

4,3̲85 ≈ [   ]

6,2̲41 ≈ [   ]

8,2̲99 ≈ [   ]

1̲,875 ≈ [   ]

5,9̲96 ≈ [   ]

7,800	200
9,800	1,200
8,800	2,200
6,800	3,200
5,800	4,200

Lesson Activities 👥

Parentheses mean "do this first!"

$(3 + 2) \times 4 =$ ☐

$3 + (2 \times 4) =$ ☐

$(16 \div 4) - 2 =$ ☐

$16 \div (4 - 2) =$ ☐

$(6 \times 7) + 1 =$ ☐

$6 \times (7 + 1) =$ ☐

4 chicken sandwiches
5 chips

$(4 \times 8) + (5 \times 3) =$ ☐

Concession Stand Menu

Chicken Sandwich.........................$8
Veggie Wrap $8
Pizza Slice $4
Hot Dog $3
Chips..$3
Bottled Water $2
Candy...$2

4 pizza slices
3 chips

5 pizza slices
1 chicken sandwich

1 veggie wrap
7 candies

2 chicken sandwiches
3 pizza slices
5 bottled waters

Practice 👤 Complete.

$(7 \times 4) + 2 = \boxed{}$
$\underbrace{}$
$\boxed{28}$

$5 \times (6 + 1) = \boxed{}$
$\boxed{}$

$(9 - 5) \times 4 = \boxed{}$

$(2 \times 10) + (3 \times 10) = \boxed{}$

$20 - (4 \times 3) = \boxed{}$

$14 \div (5 + 2) = \boxed{}$

$9 \times (2 \times 4) = \boxed{}$

$(48 \div 6) \times 6 = \boxed{}$

Use the numbers to complete the equations.

5	4

$(6 \times \boxed{}) + \boxed{} = 34$

3	10

$(\boxed{} \times 9) - \boxed{} = 87$

7	2

$(5 \times \boxed{}) + (3 \times \boxed{}) = 31$

8	6	9

★ $\boxed{} + (\boxed{} \times \boxed{}) = 78$

Review 👤 Complete.

$$89 + 1 = \boxed{}$$

$$899 + 1 = \boxed{}$$

$$8{,}999 + 1 = \boxed{}$$

$$89 + 10 = \boxed{}$$

$$899 + 10 = \boxed{}$$

$$8{,}999 + 10 = \boxed{}$$

$$80 - 1 = \boxed{}$$

$$800 - 1 = \boxed{}$$

$$8{,}000 - 1 = \boxed{}$$

$$80 - 10 = \boxed{}$$

$$800 - 10 = \boxed{}$$

$$8{,}000 - 10 = \boxed{}$$

Complete. Follow the steps.

1. Divide
2. Multiply
3. Subtract

5 | 2 2   5 | 3 2   5 | 4 2   5 | 5 2

Use the clues to complete the chart.

- Jake biked 3 times as far as Kendall.

- Jake biked 6 times as far as Aiden.

- Luna biked 5 kilometers less than Jake.

- Brynn biked twice as far as Kendall.

Name	Distance Biked
Kendall	10 km
Jake	
Aiden	
Luna	
Brynn	

Lesson Activities

Concession Stand Menu

Chicken Sandwich $8
Veggie Wrap $8
Pizza Slice $4
Hot Dog $3
Chips $3
Bottled Water $2
Candy $2

A

4 bottled waters
3 candies

Multiply, then add.

$(4 \times 2) + (3 \times 2) = \boxed{}$

Add, then multiply.

$(4 + 3) \times 2 = \boxed{}$

B

3 chicken sandwiches
7 veggie wraps

5 hot dogs
4 chips

3 chicken sandwiches
3 bottled waters

5 pizza slices
5 chips

Practice 👤 Complete. Then, match the equations with the same answer.

$(5 \times 8) + (1 \times 8) = \boxed{}$

$(4 + 5) \times 9 = \boxed{}$

$(6 \times 7) + (4 \times 7) = \boxed{}$

$(5 + 1) \times 8 = \boxed{}$

$(4 \times 8) + (4 \times 8) = \boxed{}$

$(6 + 4) \times 7 = \boxed{}$

$(4 \times 9) + (5 \times 9) = \boxed{}$

$(4 + 4) \times 8 = \boxed{}$

Complete the blanks to match the word problem. Then, solve.

Annika bought 8 boxes of chocolate chip granola bars and 2 boxes of peanut granola bars. Each box had 6 granola bars. How many granola bars did she buy?

$(\boxed{} + \boxed{}) \times \boxed{} = \boxed{}$

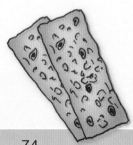

Hakeem bought 7 paperback books and 7 hardcover books at the used book sale. The paperback books cost $4 each. The hardcover books cost $6 each. How much did he pay for the books?

$(\boxed{} + \boxed{}) \times \boxed{} = \boxed{}$

Review 👤 Complete the sequences.

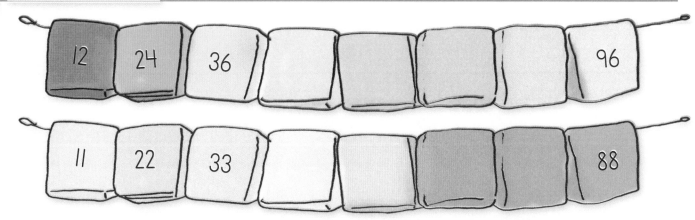

| 12 | 24 | 36 | | | | | 96 |

| 11 | 22 | 33 | | | | | 88 |

Use the diagram to answer the questions.

What is the area of the living room?

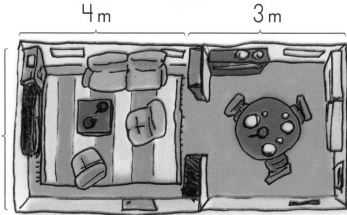

What is the area of the dining room?

What is the total area of both rooms?

Complete.

$(20 + 40) + 30 =$ ☐

$20 + (40 + 30) =$ ☐

$(50 - 30) + 20 =$ ☐

$50 - (30 + 20) =$ ☐

$(2 \times 3) \times 5 =$ ☐

$2 \times (3 \times 5) =$ ☐

Complete.

$7 \times 8 =$ ☐

$70 \times 8 =$ ☐

$7 \times 800 =$ ☐

$7 \times 8{,}000 =$ ☐

$8 \times 70 =$ ☐

$80 \times 70 =$ ☐

Lesson Activities 👥

A

3 × 11 = (3 × 10) + (3 × 1) = ☐

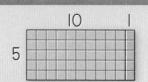

5 × 11 = (5 × 10) + (5 × 1) = ☐

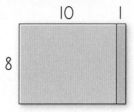

8 × 11 = ☐

6 × 11 = ☐

B

4 × 11 = ☐   9 × 11 = ☐   2 × 11 = ☐

10 × 11 = ☐   11 × 11 = ☐   12 × 11 = ☐

C

Four in a Row

11	3 × 11	10 × 11	33	5 × 11
8 × 11	12 × 11	121	2 × 11	77
44	6 × 11	110	88	9 × 11
132	99	4 × 11	11 × 11	66
1 × 11	55	7 × 11	22	11

Practice

Complete.

$2 \times 11 =$ [ ] $6 \times 11 =$ [ ] $4 \times 11 =$ [ ]

$8 \times 11 =$ [ ] $1 \times 11 =$ [ ] $9 \times 11 =$ [ ]

$3 \times 11 =$ [ ] $10 \times 11 =$ [ ] $5 \times 11 =$ [ ]

$7 \times 11 =$ [ ]   ★ $11 \times 11 =$ [ ]   ★ $12 \times 11 =$ [ ]

Use the clues to complete the chart.

- Mom is 3 times as old as Eduardo.

- Dad is 4 times as old as Eduardo.

- Grandpa is 6 times as old as Eduardo.

- Great-grandma is 8 times as old as Eduardo.

Name	Age
Eduardo	11
Mom	
Dad	
Grandpa	
Great-grandma	

Solve. Write the equations you use.

8 teams play in the soccer tournament.
Each team has 11 players.
How many players are in the tournament?

Tickets to the play cost $11.
How much does it cost to buy 6 tickets?

Review Complete the missing numbers.

$38{,}215 = \boxed{} + 8{,}000 + 200 + 10 + 5$

$96{,}760 = 90{,}000 + 6{,}000 + 700 + \boxed{}$

$149{,}304 = 100{,}000 + \boxed{} + 9{,}000 + 300 + 4$

$\boxed{} = 700{,}000 + 3{,}000 + 700 + 3$

$\boxed{} = 70{,}000 + 3{,}000 + 70 + 3$

Complete.	Color the bar to match the fraction.

$4 \times 20 = \boxed{}$

$4 \times 200 = \boxed{}$

$4 \times 2{,}000 = \boxed{}$

$40 \times 20 = \boxed{}$

$\dfrac{1}{6}$

$\dfrac{3}{6}$

$\dfrac{6}{6}$

Solve. Write the equations you use.

1,148 people came to the play on Friday. 296 fewer people came on Saturday than Friday.
How many people came on Saturday?

➡ How many people came to the play on Friday and Saturday in all?

Lesson Activities

A

10   2

4

$4 \times 12 = (4 \times 10) + (4 \times 2) = \boxed{}$

10   2

6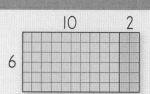

$6 \times 12 = (6 \times 10) + (6 \times 2) = \boxed{}$

10   2

5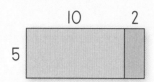

$5 \times 12 = \boxed{}$

10   2

7

$7 \times 12 = \boxed{}$

B

$3 \times 12 = \boxed{}$ $8 \times 12 = \boxed{}$ $9 \times 12 = \boxed{}$

$10 \times 12 = \boxed{}$ $11 \times 12 = \boxed{}$ $12 \times 12 = \boxed{}$

C

    # Egg Scramble

Dozens of Eggs	Number of Eggs	Dozens of Eggs	Number of Eggs
Player 1 Total		Player 2 Total	

Practice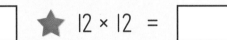

Complete.

3 × 12 = ☐   7 × 12 = ☐   4 × 12 = ☐

6 × 12 = ☐   10 × 12 = ☐   1 × 12 = ☐

2 × 12 = ☐   5 × 12 = ☐   9 × 12 = ☐

8 × 12 = ☐   ★ 11 × 12 = ☐   ★ 12 × 12 = ☐

Complete the charts.

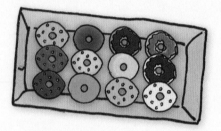

I dozen = 12 donuts

Dozens	1	3	5	8
Donuts	12			

I foot = 12 inches

Feet	2	6	10	12
Inches				

I year = 12 months

Years	4	7	9	11
Months				

Review

Complete.

$$100 - (5 \times 5) = \boxed{}$$

$$(10 \times 9) + (2 \times 9) = \boxed{}$$

$$(10 + 2) \times 9 = \boxed{}$$

Draw the missing halves for the symmetric shapes.

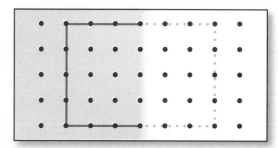

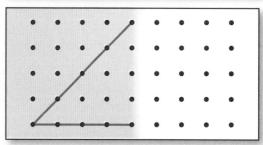

Round to the underlined place.

$450,\underline{1}28 \approx \boxed{}$

$450,\underline{7}28 \approx \boxed{}$

$7\underline{9},841 \approx \boxed{}$

$7\underline{9},341 \approx \boxed{}$

Complete. All times are p.m.

1:00	3 hr.	4:00
1:00	☐ hr.	6:00
1:30	☐ hr.	5:30
1:55	☐ hr.	5:55

Solve. Write the equations you use.

Niall bought 4 packs of cupcakes for a party.
Each pack cost $9.
He bought 3 tubs of ice cream.
Each tub cost $6.
How much did he spend in all?

Samantha mowed the lawn 6 times.
She earned $8 each time.
Then, she spent $15.
How much of her lawn-mowing money
did she have left?

Lesson Activities 👥

Area Model

10   6

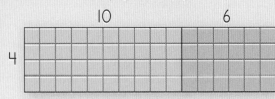

4

4 × 16 = [ ]

Box Method

10   6

4 [|]

4 × 16 = [ ]

---

10   3

5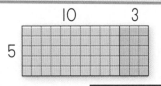

5 × 13 = [   ]

[|]

5 × 13 = [ ]

[|]

7 × 21 = [   ]

[|]

4 × 35 = [   ]

B

Roll and Multiply

Player 1	Player 2
[|]	[|]
[ ] × 34 = [ ]	[ ] × 34 = [ ]
[|]	[|]
[ ] × 42 = [ ]	[ ] × 42 = [ ]
[|]	[|]
[ ] × 91 = [ ]	[ ] × 91 = [ ]

Practice

Complete the boxes to find the product.

	10	8
3		

3 × 18 = ☐

	20	2
9		

9 × 22 = ☐

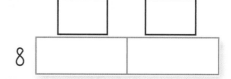

	☐	☐
6		

6 × 36 = ☐

	☐	☐
8		

8 × 47 = ☐

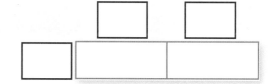

7 × 56 = ☐

9 × 99 = ☐

Find the missing numbers.

	70	4
6	420	24

☐ × ☐ = 444

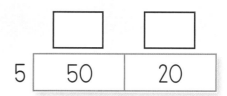

	50	20
5	50	20

5 × ☐ = 70

	30	☐
7		14

7 × ☐ = ☐

	☐	5
3	240	

☐ × ☐ = ☐

3.8

Review 👤 Complete.

$3 \times 11 =$ ☐ $\qquad$ $6 \times 11 =$ ☐ $\qquad$ $2 \times 11 =$ ☐

$7 \times 11 =$ ☐ $\qquad$ $4 \times 11 =$ ☐ $\qquad$ $8 \times 11 =$ ☐

$5 \times 11 =$ ☐ $\qquad$ $1 \times 11 =$ ☐ $\qquad$ $9 \times 11 =$ ☐

Write the word that describes all the shapes in each group.

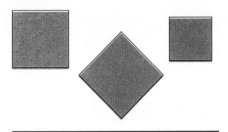

☐

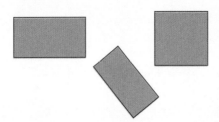

☐

rhombuses

•

rectangles

•

quadrilaterals

•

squares

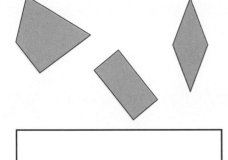

☐

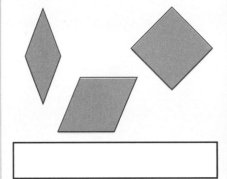

☐

Solve. Write the equations you use.

Truett has saved $12. Luke has saved
4 times as much money as Truett.
How much money has Luke saved?

Sophie has saved $50.
She has saved 5 times as much as Ellie.
How much has Ellie saved?

Lesson Activities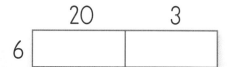

20   3

6 [|]

6 × 23 = [ ]

[|]

5 × 42 = [ ]

[|]

4 × 71 = [ ]

[|]

9 × 84 = [ ]

You buy 3 bags of marshmallows to roast at the bonfire.
There are 38 marshmallows in each bag.
How many marshmallows do you buy?

[|]

[ ] × [ ] = [ ]

You buy 5 boxes of graham crackers.
Each box has 27 crackers.
How many crackers do you buy?

[|]

[ ] × [ ] = [ ]

You buy 36 chocolate bars.
Each bar has 4 pieces of chocolate.
How many pieces of chocolate do you buy?

[|]

[ ] × [ ] = [ ]

Practice 👤 Complete the boxes to solve the problems.

Ethan buys 6 boxes of cookies.
Each box has 24 cookies.
How many cookies does he buy?

6 × 24 = ☐

June earns $27 per hour.
She works for 7 hours.
How much money does she earn?

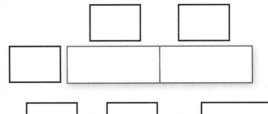

☐ × ☐ = ☐

On Monday, Benjamin reads 48 pages in his book. On Tuesday, he reads 4 times as many pages as on Monday.
How many pages does he read on Tuesday?

☐ × ☐ = ☐

The chairs at the concert are arranged in 6 rows. There are 48 chairs in each row.
How many chairs are there in all?

☐ × ☐ = ☐

Complete the boxes to find the area.

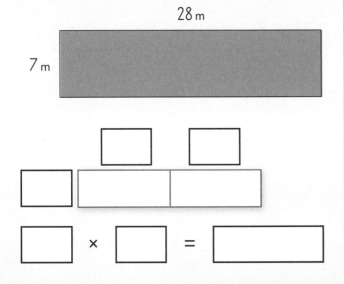

28 m

7 m

☐ × ☐ = ☐

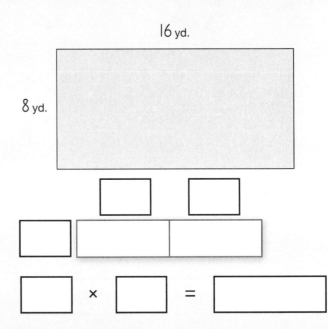

16 yd.

8 yd.

☐ × ☐ = ☐

Review 👤 Complete.

$4 \times 12 = $ ☐ $2 \times 12 = $ ☐ $9 \times 12 = $ ☐

$6 \times 12 = $ ☐ $5 \times 12 = $ ☐ $3 \times 12 = $ ☐

$1 \times 12 = $ ☐ $8 \times 12 = $ ☐ $7 \times 12 = $ ☐

Use a ruler to measure.

cm   cm   cm

Match each number to its dot on the number line.

| 137,419 | 137,250 | 137,806 | 137,723 |

137,000   138,000

Solve. Write the equations you use.

Ella buys 8 packs of pencils.
Each pack has 12 pencils.
How many pencils does she buy?

Nathan buys 9 packs of pens. Each pack has 10 black pens and 1 red pen. How many pens does he buy?

Unit Wrap-Up 👤

Madison made a bar graph to show how long she practiced her flute each day. Use the clues to complete her graph.

- Madison practiced 20 minutes on Monday.

- She practiced 10 minutes less on Tuesday than Monday.

- She practiced 5 times as long on Wednesday as she did on Tuesday.

- She practiced 3 times as long on Thursday as she did on Monday.

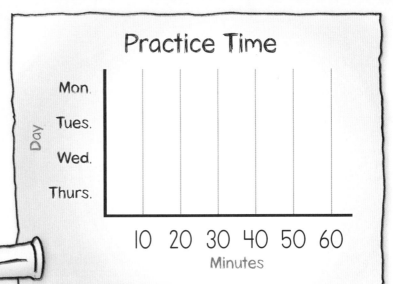

Complete.

$7 \times 11 =$ ☐ $5 \times 12 =$ ☐ $9 \times 11 =$ ☐

$8 \times 12 =$ ☐ $8 \times 11 =$ ☐ $7 \times 12 =$ ☐

$6 \times 11 =$ ☐ $9 \times 12 =$ ☐ $6 \times 12 =$ ☐

Color the problems that equal the number in the star.

240	400	1,200	1,800
8 × 30	2 × 200	4 × 30	9 × 200
5 × 60	8 × 50	4 × 300	4 × 500
6 × 40	4 × 10	6 × 200	6 × 300
60 × 40	20 × 20	40 × 30	20 × 90

Unit Wrap-Up 👤 **Complete.**

$70 - (9 \times 7) = \boxed{}$

$(6 \times 5) + 18 = \boxed{}$

$(9 \times 8) + (1 \times 8) = \boxed{}$

$(9 + 1) \times 8 = \boxed{}$

Complete the boxes to solve.

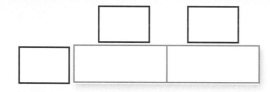

$6 \times 45 = \boxed{}$

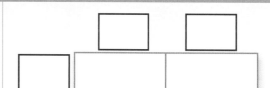

$4 \times 91 = \boxed{}$

$5 \times 87 = \boxed{}$

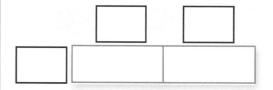

$7 \times 21 = \boxed{}$

Solve. Write the equations you use.

Gavin has 4 balls of purple clay and 5 balls of green clay.
Each ball weighs 8 ounces.
How many ounces of clay does he have?

Jerome has played the violin for 4 years.
How many months has he played the violin?

Lesson Activities 👥

Numerator
Number of parts

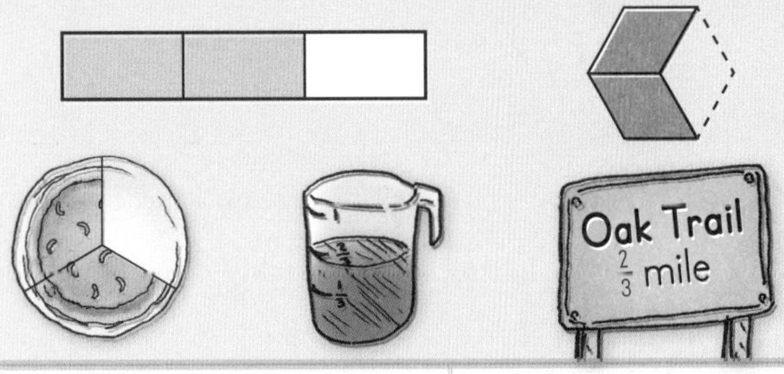

$$\frac{2}{3}$$

Denominator
How many equal parts
the whole was split into

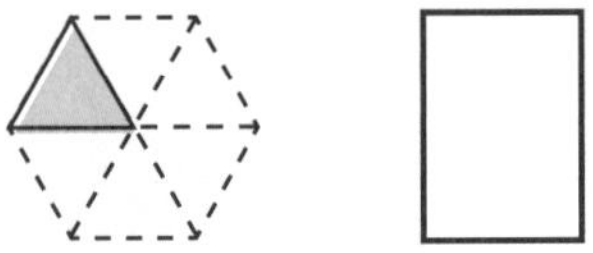

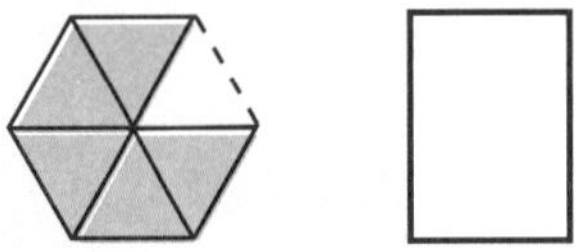

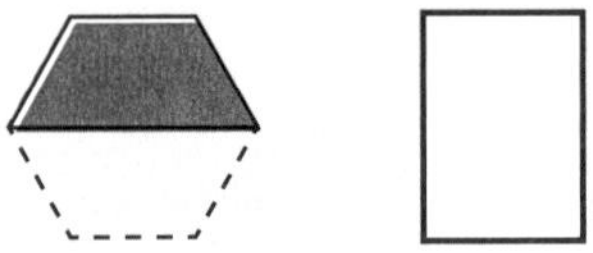

Oak Trail
$\frac{2}{3}$ mile

$\frac{0}{2}$　　　　　　$\frac{1}{2}$　　　　　　$\frac{2}{2}$

0　　　　　　　　　　　　　　1

0

0

0

0

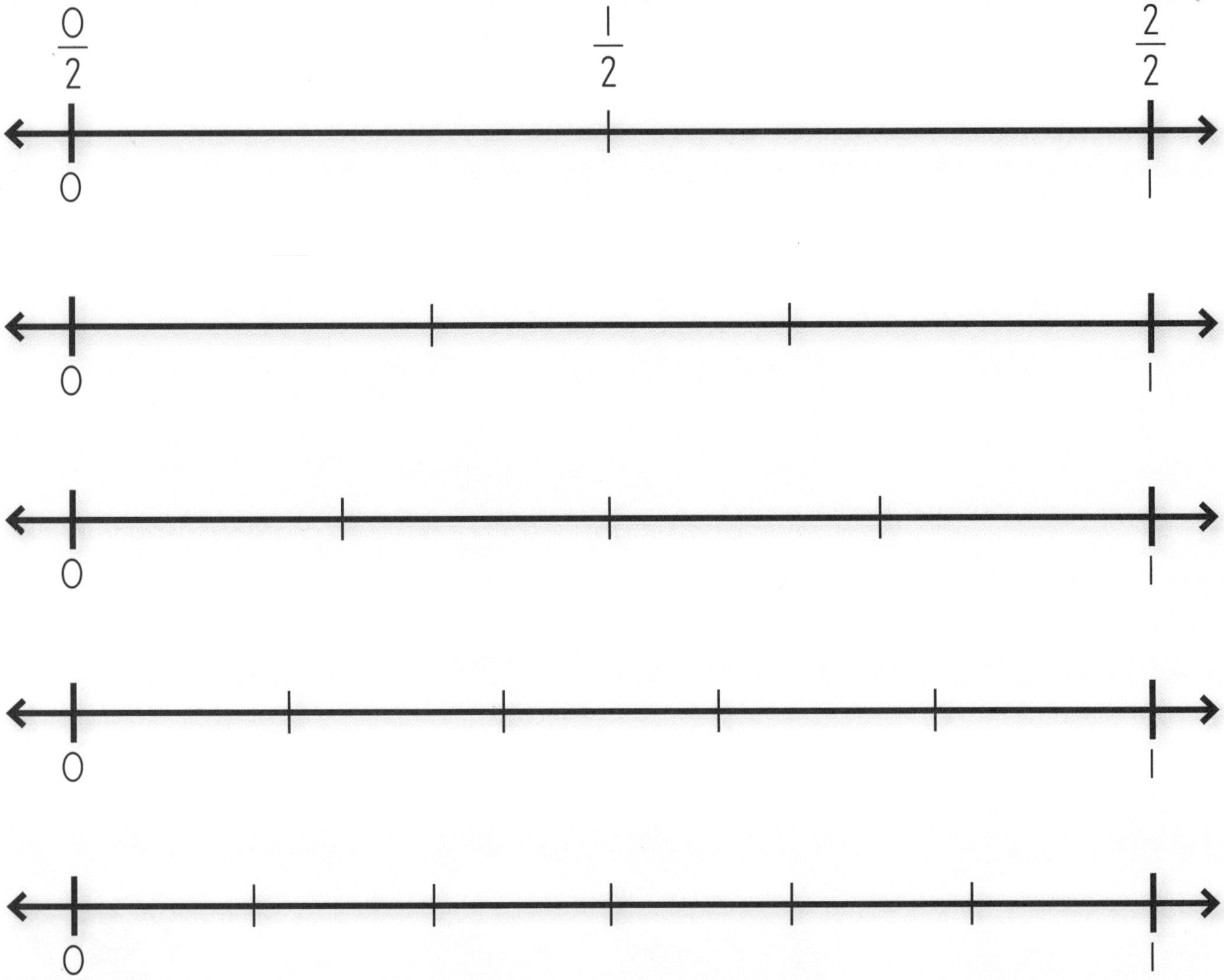

Practice

Match pairs of fractions that equal 1 whole.

$\frac{1}{6}$ $\frac{1}{8}$ $\frac{1}{3}$ $\frac{1}{4}$ $\frac{1}{2}$

$\frac{2}{3}$ $\frac{7}{8}$

$\frac{5}{6}$ $\frac{1}{2}$ $\frac{3}{4}$

Label the missing fractions on the number lines.
Then, use the number lines to complete the circles with <, >, or =.

$\frac{0}{4}$ ▢ ▢ ▢ $\frac{4}{4}$

0 | | | 1

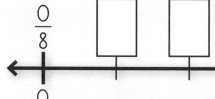

$\frac{0}{8}$ ▢ ▢ $\frac{3}{8}$ ▢ $\frac{5}{8}$ $\frac{6}{8}$ ▢ ▢

0 1

$\frac{1}{4}$ ◯ $\frac{1}{8}$ $\frac{3}{8}$ ◯ $\frac{4}{8}$ $\frac{4}{4}$ ◯ $\frac{8}{8}$

$\frac{1}{4}$ ◯ $\frac{0}{4}$ $\frac{2}{4}$ ◯ $\frac{4}{8}$ $\frac{7}{8}$ ◯ $\frac{3}{4}$

4.1

Review

Complete.

8 × 11 = ☐   8 × 12 = ☐

7 × 11 = ☐   7 × 12 = ☐

5 × 11 = ☐   5 × 12 = ☐

9 × 11 = ☐   9 × 12 = ☐

Complete with <, >, or =.

275,346 ◯ 25,346

408,752 ◯ 409,752

382,070 ◯ 382,700

974,206 ◯ 974,206

Complete. All times are a.m.

8:00	← 1 hr.	9:00
☐	← 2 hr.	9:00
☐	← 4 hr.	9:00
☐	← 8 hr.	9:00
☐	← 9 hr.	9:00

Complete.

2,500 + 500 = ☐

4,500 + 1,500 = ☐

3,500 + 4,500 = ☐

7,500 + 2,500 = ☐

9,500 + 3,500 = ☐

Solve. Write the equations you use.

George keeps his baseball cards in plastic sleeves. 9 cards fit in each sleeve.
If he buys 63 baseball cards, how many sleeves will he fill?

Four friends have a lemonade stand.
They earn $32 in all.
If they split the money evenly, how much does each person get?

Lesson Activities

Mixed Number

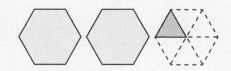

$$2 + \frac{1}{6} = 2\frac{1}{6}$$

↑ Whole Number   ↑ Fraction

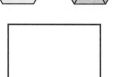

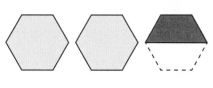

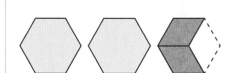

B

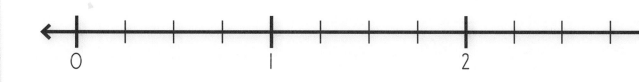

C

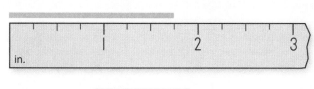

 in.

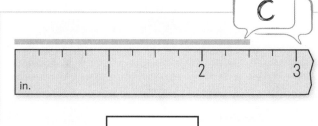

 in.

cm

cm

Practice 👤 Match each fraction or mixed number to its place on the number line.

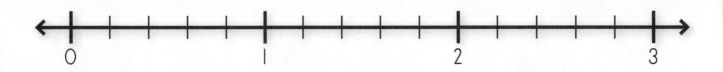

$1\frac{1}{5}$ $\frac{3}{5}$ $1\frac{3}{5}$ $2\frac{4}{5}$ $2\frac{2}{5}$

$1\frac{2}{3}$ $2\frac{1}{3}$ $1\frac{1}{3}$ $3\frac{1}{3}$ $2\frac{2}{3}$

Write each length as a mixed number.

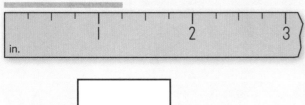

[ ] in.

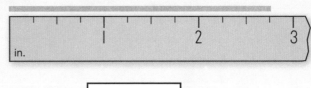

[ ] in.

[ ] cm

[ ] cm

Review

Complete the boxes to find the product.

	30	8
5		

5 × 38 = ☐

4 × 73 = ☐

7 × 81 = ☐

9 × 64 = ☐

Copy the triangles.

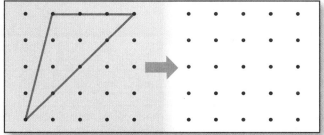

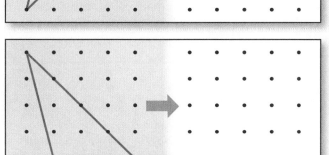

Complete.

10 ÷ 3 = 3 R1

11 ÷ 3 = ☐

12 ÷ 3 = ☐

13 ÷ 3 = ☐

14 ÷ 3 = ☐

15 ÷ 3 = ☐

Solve. Write the equations you use.

Chloe collects stuffed bears.
She has 3 polar bears. She has 6 times as many panda bears as polar bears.
How many panda bears does she have?

Sullivan collects coins.
He has 30 European coins. He has 5 times as many European coins as Asian coins.
How many Asian coins does he have?

4.3

Lesson Activities

A

Mixed Number   Improper Fraction

$$1\frac{3}{8} = \frac{11}{8}$$

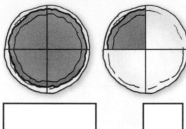

$\boxed{} = \boxed{}$

$\boxed{} = \boxed{}$

$\boxed{} = \boxed{}$

B

$\boxed{\frac{}{2}}$ $\boxed{\frac{}{3}}$ $\boxed{\frac{}{6}}$

$\boxed{\frac{}{2}}$ $\boxed{\frac{}{3}}$ $\boxed{\frac{}{6}}$

$\boxed{\frac{}{2}}$ $\boxed{\frac{}{3}}$ $\boxed{\frac{}{6}}$

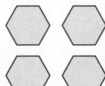

$\boxed{\frac{}{2}}$ $\boxed{\frac{}{3}}$ $\boxed{\frac{}{6}}$

C

Fraction Crash

$\frac{12}{6}$	$\frac{6}{2}$	$\frac{12}{3}$	$\frac{3}{3}$	$\frac{4}{2}$	$\frac{6}{6}$
$\frac{6}{3}$	$\frac{24}{6}$	$\frac{2}{2}$	$\frac{18}{6}$	$\frac{9}{3}$	$\frac{8}{2}$

Practice 👤 **Complete with a fraction.**

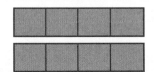

2 wholes = ☐ fourths

$2 = \dfrac{}{4}$

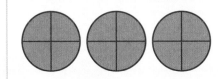

3 wholes = ☐ fourths

$3 = \dfrac{}{4}$

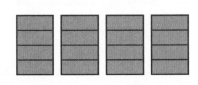

4 wholes = ☐ fourths

$4 = \dfrac{}{4}$

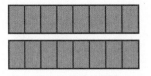

$2 = \dfrac{}{8}$

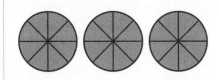

$3 = \dfrac{}{8}$

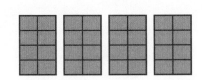

$4 = \dfrac{}{8}$

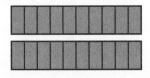

$2 = \dfrac{}{10}$

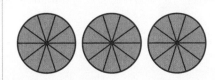

$3 = \dfrac{}{10}$

$4 = \dfrac{}{10}$

Solve.

Brandon has 2 chocolate bars.
He breaks each chocolate bar into eighths.
How many pieces does he have?

Gabriel makes 3 loaves of banana bread.
He cuts each loaf into sixths. How many
slices of banana bread does he have?

Review 👤 Complete. Follow the steps.

| 1. Divide |
| 2. Multiply |
| 3. Subtract |

3 ⌐2 9   4 ⌐2 9   5 ⌐2 9   6 ⌐2 9

Round to the underlined place.

47,9<u>6</u>5 ≈ [　　　]

32,<u>7</u>53 ≈ [　　　]

9<u>8</u>,564 ≈ [　　　]

205,<u>4</u>99 ≈ [　　　]

356,<u>0</u>78 ≈ [　　　]

Complete.

9 × 40 = [　　　]

8 × 600 = [　　　]

7 × 7,000 = [　　　]

90 × 80 = [　　　]

6 × 9,000 = [　　　]

Find the perimeter and area.

12 m

5 m [　　]

Perimeter: [　　] m

Area: [　　] sq. m

6 yd.

11 yd. [　　]

Perimeter: [　　] yd.

Area: [　　] sq. yd.

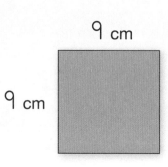

9 cm

9 cm [　　]

Perimeter: [　　] cm

Area: [　　] sq. cm

Lesson Activities 👥

   $\dfrac{}{4}$ $\dfrac{}{5}$ $\dfrac{}{8}$ $\dfrac{}{10}$ $\dfrac{}{12}$

Fraction	$\frac{1}{3}$	$\frac{2}{3}$	$\frac{3}{3}$	$\frac{4}{3}$	$\frac{5}{3}$	$\frac{6}{3}$	$\frac{7}{3}$	$\frac{8}{3}$	$\frac{9}{3}$
Whole or Mixed Number									

$\frac{0}{3}$ $\frac{1}{3}$ $\frac{2}{3}$ $\frac{3}{3}$ $\frac{4}{3}$ $\frac{5}{3}$ $\frac{6}{3}$ $\frac{7}{3}$ $\frac{8}{3}$ $\frac{9}{3}$

←———————————————————————→

Pizza Roll

Player 1

Player 2
   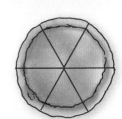

Practice

Color the bars to match the mixed numbers. Then, write each mixed number as a fraction.

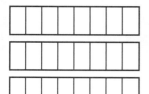

$2\frac{1}{8} = \boxed{}$

$2\frac{2}{3} = \boxed{}$

$2\frac{4}{5} = \boxed{}$

Color the bars to match the fractions. Then, write each fraction as a mixed number or whole number.

$\frac{20}{8} = \boxed{}$

$\frac{6}{2} = \boxed{}$

$\frac{14}{6} = \boxed{}$

$\frac{12}{4} = \boxed{}$

$\frac{7}{3} = \boxed{}$

$\frac{15}{5} = \boxed{}$

Solve.

Fiona has $2\frac{1}{2}$ sandwiches. How many halves of a sandwich does she have?

Steven's family has $2\frac{5}{6}$ pies.
Each pie is cut in sixths.
How many slices do they have?

Review

Complete.

$42 \div 6 =$ ☐

$42 \div 7 =$ ☐

$56 \div 8 =$ ☐

$56 \div 7 =$ ☐

Complete.

$(7 + 4) \times 11 =$ ☐

$(3 \times 9) + (7 \times 9) =$ ☐

$60 - (8 \times 7) =$ ☐

$(6 \times 6) + (8 \times 8) =$ ☐

Write the time.

Draw the missing halves for the symmetric shapes.

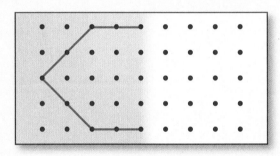
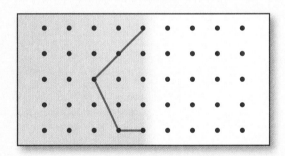

Solve. Write the equations you use.

Maria has 78 trading cards.
Then, she buys 4 new packs.
Each pack has 8 cards.
How many trading cards does she have now?

Sam buys 9 packs of trading cards.
Each pack has 8 cards.
Then, he gives 17 of the cards to a friend.
How many trading cards does he have now?

Lesson Activities 👥

A

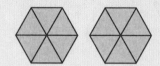

$$2 = \boxed{\frac{}{6}}$$

$$2 \times 6 = \boxed{}$$

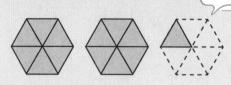

$$2\frac{1}{6} = \boxed{\frac{}{6}}$$

$$(2 \times 6) + 1 = \boxed{}$$

$$3 = \boxed{\frac{}{2}}$$

$$3\frac{1}{2} = \boxed{\frac{}{2}}$$

$$2 = \boxed{\frac{}{3}}$$

$$2\frac{2}{3} = \boxed{\frac{}{3}}$$

$$3 = \boxed{\frac{}{4}}$$

$$3\frac{1}{4} = \boxed{\frac{}{4}}$$

B

Fraction Three in a Row

| Player 1 START | $5\frac{1}{2}$ | $1\frac{7}{8}$ | $5\frac{3}{4}$ | $4\frac{1}{3}$ | $3\frac{5}{8}$ |

$4\frac{1}{6}$

$3\frac{2}{3}$

$3\frac{1}{4}$

$1\frac{5}{6}$

Circles:
$\frac{17}{6}$ $\frac{11}{3}$ $\frac{29}{8}$ $\frac{13}{3}$

$\frac{19}{8}$ $\frac{15}{8}$ $\frac{25}{6}$ $\frac{13}{5}$

$\frac{15}{4}$ $\frac{13}{4}$ $\frac{11}{2}$ $\frac{17}{3}$

$\frac{11}{6}$ $\frac{23}{4}$ $\frac{19}{4}$ $\frac{13}{10}$

$1\frac{3}{10}$

$2\frac{5}{6}$

$5\frac{2}{3}$

| $1\frac{5}{6}$ | $2\frac{3}{5}$ | $2\frac{3}{8}$ | $3\frac{3}{4}$ | $4\frac{3}{4}$ | Player 2 START |

Practice

Color the bars to match each whole number or mixed number. Then, convert the number to a fraction.

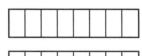

$1\dfrac{3}{8} = \boxed{}$

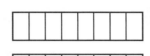

$2 = \boxed{}$

$2\dfrac{7}{8} = \boxed{}$

$1\dfrac{2}{5} = \boxed{}$

$2 = \boxed{}$

$2\dfrac{3}{5} = \boxed{}$

Write each mixed number as a fraction.

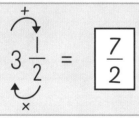

$3\dfrac{1}{2} = \boxed{\dfrac{7}{2}}$

$4\dfrac{1}{2} = \boxed{}$

$7\dfrac{1}{2} = \boxed{}$

$2\dfrac{1}{4} = \boxed{}$

$3\dfrac{3}{4} = \boxed{}$

$5\dfrac{1}{4} = \boxed{}$

$2\dfrac{1}{6} = \boxed{}$

$4\dfrac{5}{6} = \boxed{}$

$5\dfrac{2}{6} = \boxed{}$

Review 👤 Complete the missing fractions on the number lines.

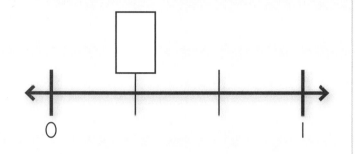

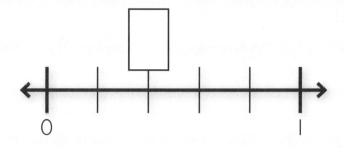

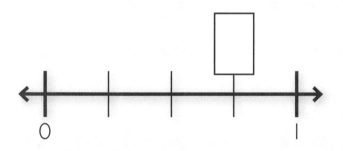

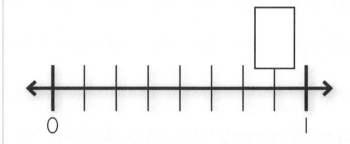

Complete the boxes to find the product.

```
       30          8
   8 ┌──────┬──────┐
     │      │      │
     └──────┴──────┘
```

8 × 38 = [ ]

```
   ┌──────┬──────┐
   │      │      │
   └──────┴──────┘
```

7 × 65 = [ ]

Solve. Write the equations you use.

Charis' family picks 56 apples.
They put 8 apples in each bag.
How many bags do they fill?

Carson's family buys 3 boxes of donuts.
There are 12 donuts in each box.
How many donuts do they buy?

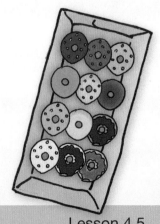

Lesson Activities

A

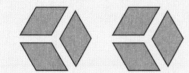

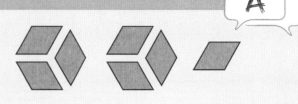

$\frac{6}{3}$ = ☐

$6 \div 3$ = ☐

$\frac{7}{3}$ = ☐

$7 \div 3$ = ☐

$\frac{11}{3}$ = ☐

$\frac{13}{6}$ = ☐

$\frac{8}{2}$ = ☐

$\frac{9}{4}$ = ☐

$\frac{19}{8}$ = ☐

$\frac{8}{5}$ = ☐

B

Fraction Three in a Row

Player 1 START	$\frac{27}{10}$	$\frac{11}{8}$	$\frac{6}{6}$	$\frac{9}{5}$	$\frac{13}{4}$
$\frac{5}{2}$	$3\frac{1}{3}$	$1\frac{4}{5}$	2	$1\frac{3}{10}$	$\frac{5}{3}$
$\frac{10}{3}$	1	$3\frac{1}{4}$	$2\frac{1}{6}$	4	$\frac{8}{2}$
$\frac{9}{4}$	$3\frac{1}{8}$	$2\frac{7}{10}$	$1\frac{3}{8}$	$1\frac{5}{6}$	$\frac{11}{6}$
$\frac{15}{5}$	$2\frac{1}{2}$	3	$2\frac{1}{4}$	$1\frac{2}{3}$	Player 2 START
	$\frac{13}{6}$	$\frac{25}{8}$	$\frac{13}{10}$	$\frac{8}{4}$	

Practice

Color the bars to match each fraction.
Then, write the fraction as a whole number or mixed number.

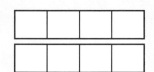

$\dfrac{7}{4}$ = _____

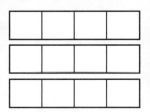

$\dfrac{8}{4}$ = _____

$\dfrac{9}{4}$ = _____

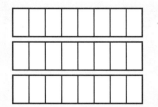

$\dfrac{17}{8}$ = _____

$\dfrac{15}{6}$ = _____

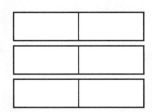

$\dfrac{5}{2}$ = _____

Write each fraction as a whole number or mixed number.

$\div\ \dfrac{9}{8}$ = $1\dfrac{1}{8}$

$\dfrac{5}{4}$ = _____

$\dfrac{12}{6}$ = _____

$\dfrac{11}{5}$ = _____

$\dfrac{7}{2}$ = _____

$\dfrac{8}{3}$ = _____

$\dfrac{11}{4}$ = _____

$\dfrac{18}{3}$ = _____

$\dfrac{13}{8}$ = _____

Review : **Match the fractions and mixed numbers to their places on the number line.**

| $\frac{20}{8}$ | $\frac{23}{8}$ | $\frac{29}{8}$ | $\frac{25}{8}$ |

$\frac{16}{8}$ $\frac{24}{8}$ $\frac{32}{8}$

2   3   4

| $2\frac{7}{8}$ | $3\frac{1}{8}$ | $2\frac{4}{8}$ | $3\frac{5}{8}$ |

Complete.

$49 \div 7 = \boxed{}$ $48 \div 8 = \boxed{}$ $81 \div 9 = \boxed{}$

$42 \div 7 = \boxed{}$ $64 \div 8 = \boxed{}$ $54 \div 9 = \boxed{}$

$56 \div 7 = \boxed{}$ $56 \div 8 = \boxed{}$ $72 \div 9 = \boxed{}$

$63 \div 7 = \boxed{}$ $72 \div 8 = \boxed{}$ $63 \div 9 = \boxed{}$

Complete.

4 weeks = $\boxed{}$ days   35 days = $\boxed{}$ weeks

4 weeks, 2 days = $\boxed{}$ days   38 days = $\boxed{}$ weeks, $\boxed{}$ days

12 weeks = $\boxed{}$ days   42 days = $\boxed{}$ weeks

12 weeks, 1 day = $\boxed{}$ days   45 days = $\boxed{}$ weeks, $\boxed{}$ days

4.7

Lesson Activities 👥

A

$$\frac{2}{6} + \frac{3}{6} = \boxed{}$$

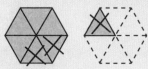

$$\frac{7}{6} - \frac{3}{6} = \boxed{}$$

$$\frac{5}{3} + \frac{2}{3} = \boxed{}$$

$$\frac{3}{8} + \frac{4}{8} = \boxed{}$$

$$\frac{4}{2} - \frac{1}{2} = \boxed{}$$

$$\frac{6}{4} - \frac{3}{4} = \boxed{}$$

B

Climb and Slide

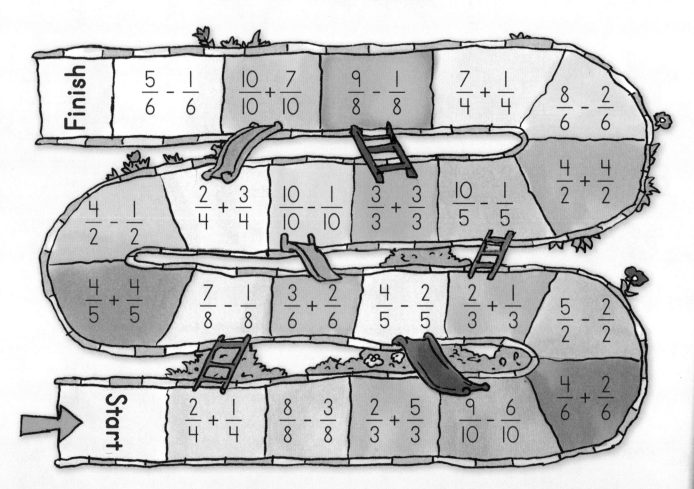

Lesson 4.7

Practice

Complete with a fraction. Color the bars to match.

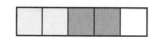

$\frac{2}{5} + \frac{2}{5} = \boxed{}$

$\frac{5}{8} + \frac{3}{8} = \boxed{}$

$\frac{1}{6} + \frac{4}{6} = \boxed{}$

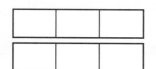

$\frac{2}{3} + \frac{2}{3} = \boxed{}$

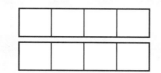

$\frac{5}{4} + \frac{3}{4} = \boxed{}$

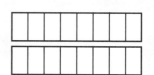

$\frac{8}{8} + \frac{7}{8} = \boxed{}$

Complete with a fraction. X the bars to match.

$\frac{4}{5} - \frac{1}{5} = \boxed{}$

$\frac{5}{8} - \frac{2}{8} = \boxed{}$

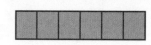

$\frac{6}{6} - \frac{6}{6} = \boxed{}$

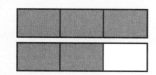

$\frac{5}{3} - \frac{3}{3} = \boxed{}$

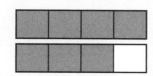

$\frac{7}{4} - \frac{5}{4} = \boxed{}$

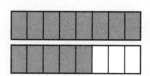

$\frac{13}{8} - \frac{5}{8} = \boxed{}$

Complete.

Jacob runs around the track 5 times. Each lap is $\frac{1}{4}$ of a mile.

• Write how far Jacob runs as a fraction.

• Write how far Jacob runs as a mixed number.

Review 👤 **Convert the mixed numbers to fractions.**
Convert the fractions to mixed numbers or whole numbers.

$5\frac{1}{2}$ = ☐ $3\frac{2}{3}$ = ☐ $5\frac{3}{4}$ = ☐

$\frac{17}{5}$ = ☐ $\frac{25}{6}$ = ☐ $\frac{16}{5}$ = ☐

Write a fraction or mixed number for each length.

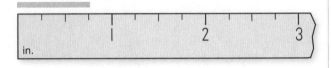

☐ in.

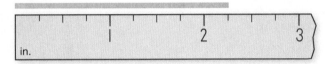

☐ in.

☐ cm

☐ cm

Solve. Write the equations you use.

Josephine's family is buying a new car. The car costs $35,789, plus $2,147 in sales tax. How much does the car cost in all?

The art museum is raising money for a new exhibit. The goal is $50,000. So far, they have raised $27,900. How much more money do they need?

Lesson Activities 👥

Repeated Addition

$$\frac{1}{6} + \frac{1}{6} + \frac{1}{6} + \frac{1}{6} = \boxed{}$$

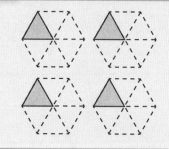

Multiplication

$$4 \times \frac{1}{6} = \boxed{}$$

$$2 \times \frac{1}{3} = \boxed{}$$

$$5 \times \frac{1}{6} = \boxed{}$$

$$3 \times \frac{1}{4} = \boxed{}$$

$$4 \times \frac{2}{6} = \boxed{} = \boxed{}$$

$$3 \times \frac{1}{2} = \boxed{} = \boxed{}$$

$$3 \times \frac{3}{8} = \boxed{} = \boxed{}$$

Roll and Multiply

Player 1	Player 2
$\boxed{} \times \frac{1}{6} = \boxed{} = \boxed{}$	$\boxed{} \times \frac{1}{6} = \boxed{} = \boxed{}$
$\boxed{} \times \frac{1}{3} = \boxed{} = \boxed{}$	$\boxed{} \times \frac{1}{3} = \boxed{} = \boxed{}$
$\boxed{} \times \frac{1}{2} = \boxed{} = \boxed{}$	$\boxed{} \times \frac{1}{2} = \boxed{} = \boxed{}$
$\boxed{} \times \frac{2}{3} = \boxed{} = \boxed{}$	$\boxed{} \times \frac{2}{3} = \boxed{} = \boxed{}$
$\boxed{} \times \frac{3}{2} = \boxed{} = \boxed{}$	$\boxed{} \times \frac{3}{2} = \boxed{} = \boxed{}$

Practice 👤 Write a fraction to complete each equation.

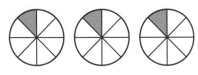

$3 \times \dfrac{1}{8} = \boxed{}$

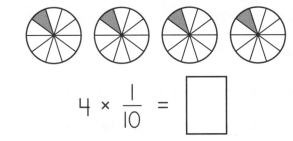

$4 \times \dfrac{1}{10} = \boxed{}$

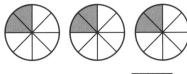

$3 \times \dfrac{2}{8} = \boxed{}$

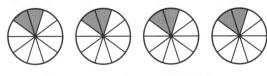

$4 \times \dfrac{2}{10} = \boxed{}$

**Write a fraction to complete each equation.
Then, convert the fraction to a mixed number or a whole number.**

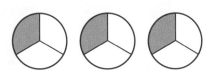

$3 \times \dfrac{1}{3} = \boxed{} = \boxed{}$

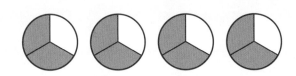

$4 \times \dfrac{2}{3} = \boxed{} = \boxed{}$

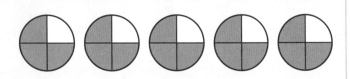

$5 \times \dfrac{3}{4} = \boxed{} = \boxed{}$

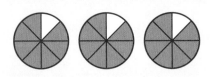

$3 \times \dfrac{7}{8} = \boxed{} = \boxed{}$

$2 \times \dfrac{5}{6} = \boxed{} = \boxed{}$

$8 \times \dfrac{1}{2} = \boxed{} = \boxed{}$

Review Complete.

	2	9	0	,	6	8	4
+	3	4	5	,	1	2	5

	8	7	6	,	9	8	5
−	6	8	4	,	9	2	0

Choose the more sensible unit for each item.

Weight of an egg

2 oz.	2 lb.

Weight of a new baby

7 oz.	7 lb.

Weight of a dumbbell

8 g	8 kg

Capacity of an aquarium

8 c.	8 gal.

Capacity of a bathtub

50 c.	50 gal.

Capacity of a watering can

6 mL	6 L

Complete with a fraction.

$$\frac{2}{3} + \frac{5}{3} = \boxed{}$$

$$\frac{4}{8} + \frac{5}{8} = \boxed{}$$

$$\frac{10}{10} - \frac{3}{10} = \boxed{}$$

Complete.

$7 \times 11 = \boxed{}$ $7 \times 12 = \boxed{}$

$4 \times 11 = \boxed{}$ $4 \times 12 = \boxed{}$

$6 \times 11 = \boxed{}$ $6 \times 12 = \boxed{}$

$8 \times 11 = \boxed{}$ $8 \times 12 = \boxed{}$

Lesson Activities 👥

A

Mixed Number Addition Algorithm

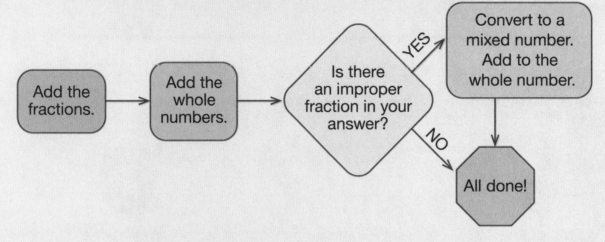

Add the fractions. → Add the whole numbers. → Is there an improper fraction in your answer? —YES→ Convert to a mixed number. Add to the whole number. → All done!
—NO→ All done!

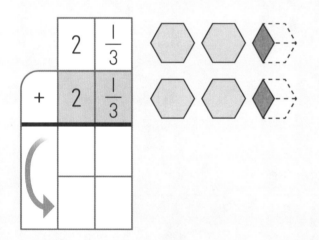

$$\begin{array}{c} 2\frac{1}{3} \\ +\ 2\frac{1}{3} \\ \hline \end{array}$$

$$\begin{array}{c} 3\frac{1}{2} \\ +\ 1\frac{1}{2} \\ \hline \end{array}$$

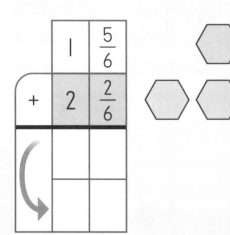

$$\begin{array}{c} 1\frac{5}{6} \\ +\ 2\frac{2}{6} \\ \hline \end{array}$$

$$\begin{array}{c} 1\frac{5}{8} \\ +\ 2\frac{5}{8} \\ \hline \end{array}$$

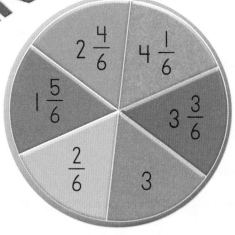

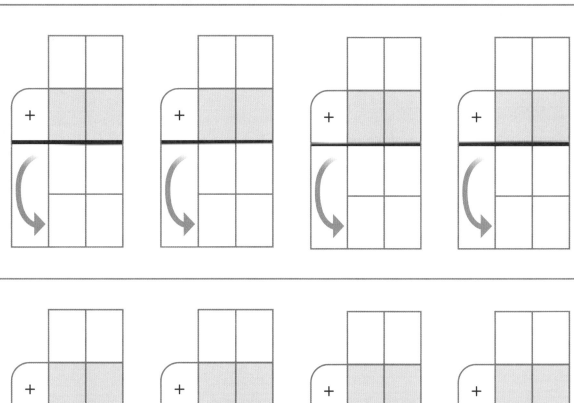

Practice 👤 Complete.

2	$\frac{3}{8}$
+ 4	$\frac{7}{8}$

2	$\frac{7}{10}$
+ 1	$\frac{2}{10}$

6	$\frac{3}{4}$
+ 2	$\frac{2}{4}$

3	$\frac{3}{5}$
+ 2	$\frac{2}{5}$

Review 👤 Write a fraction to complete each equation. Then, convert the fraction to a mixed number or whole number.

$$4 \times \frac{2}{5} = \boxed{\frac{8}{5}} = \boxed{1\frac{3}{5}}$$

$$2 \times \frac{4}{6} = \boxed{} = \boxed{}$$

$$3 \times \frac{3}{8} = \boxed{} = \boxed{}$$

$$6 \times \frac{2}{3} = \boxed{} = \boxed{}$$

Use the clues to find the secret number.

- The number has 6 digits.

- There is a 5 in the thousands place.

- There is a 6 in the ten thousands place.

- The sum of the digit in the tens place and the digit in the thousands place is 8.

- The product of the digit in the tens place and the digit in the ones place is 27.

- The digit in the ones place is the same as the digit in the hundreds place.

- The number is greater than 400,000 and less than 500,000.

Secret Number: ☐ ☐ ☐ ☐ ☐ ☐

Lesson Activities 👥

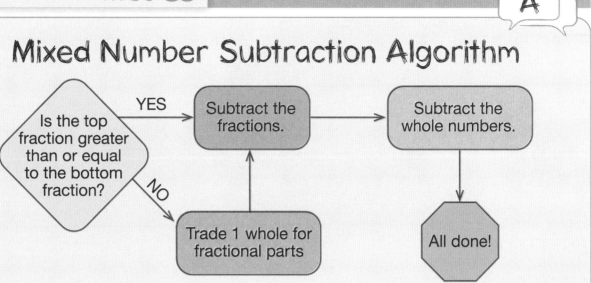

Mixed Number Subtraction Algorithm

Is the top fraction greater than or equal to the bottom fraction? — **YES** → Subtract the fractions. → Subtract the whole numbers. → All done!

NO → Trade 1 whole for fractional parts → Subtract the fractions.

	2	$\frac{5}{6}$
−	1	$\frac{1}{6}$

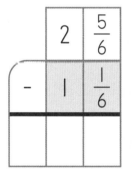

	3	
−	1	$\frac{2}{3}$

	2	$\frac{1}{6}$
−		$\frac{5}{6}$

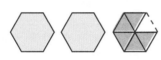

	5	$\frac{1}{4}$
−	2	$\frac{3}{4}$

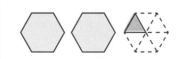

SPIN TO WIN!

Spinner 1: $4\frac{3}{6}$, 4, $3\frac{2}{6}$, $3\frac{1}{6}$, 3, $3\frac{5}{6}$

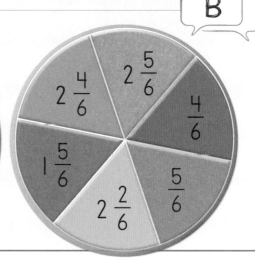

Spinner 2: $2\frac{5}{6}$, $2\frac{4}{6}$, $4\frac{6}{6}$, $1\frac{5}{6}$, $2\frac{2}{6}$, $\frac{5}{6}$

Player 1

$-$

$-$

$-$

$-$

Player 2

$-$

$-$

$-$

$-$

Practice   Complete.

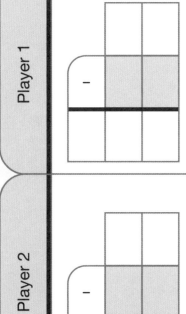

4
$-\ 2\ \frac{2}{3}$

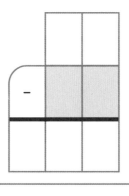

$4\ \frac{2}{10}$
$-\ 3\ \frac{5}{10}$

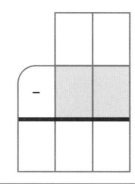

$5\ \frac{1}{6}$
$-\ 2\ \frac{4}{6}$

$3\ \frac{7}{8}$
$-\ 1\ \frac{3}{8}$

Review

Color the multiples in order from Start to End.

Multiples of 11

Start → 11	22	33	36	40
17	24	44	45	42
21	48	55	66	72
30	56	60	77	110 **END**
36	63	72	88	99

Multiples of 12

24	36	42	64	80
Start → 12	48	60	72	77
8	56	54	84	92
4	16	40	96	108
6	20	28	110	120 **END**

Complete.

400,000 + 27,000 = ☐   8 × 3,000 = ☐

125,000 + 125,000 = ☐   7 × 6,000 = ☐

76,000 + 4,000 = ☐   8 × 8,000 = ☐

100,000 − 10,000 = ☐   4 × 5,000 = ☐

500,000 − 50,000 = ☐   9 × 10,000 = ☐

Complete the missing mixed numbers.

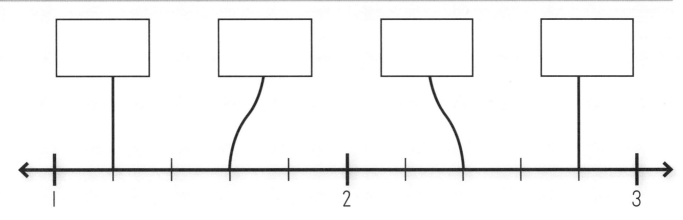

Lesson Activities

A

$4 = \dfrac{\boxed{}}{5}$ $2\dfrac{1}{8} = \boxed{}$ $\dfrac{11}{4} = \boxed{}$

$5 \times \dfrac{3}{4} = \boxed{} = \boxed{}$

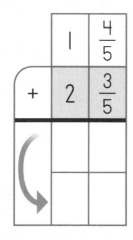

B

Emmett's mom uses $3\dfrac{1}{8}$ pounds of red apples and $1\dfrac{6}{8}$ pounds of green apples to make applesauce. How many pounds of apples does she use in all?

Jai has 4 quarts of juice. He uses $2\dfrac{7}{8}$ quarts to make punch. How much juice is left?

Stella uses $\dfrac{1}{4}$ meter of ribbon for each bow. How many meters of ribbon does she need to make 9 bows?

The Meadow hiking trail is $3\dfrac{7}{10}$ kilometers long. The Highlands trail is $2\dfrac{4}{10}$ kilometers long. How much longer is the Meadow trail than the Highlands trail?

Practice 👤 Complete.

	2	$\frac{3}{8}$
+	4	$\frac{7}{8}$

	2	$\frac{2}{5}$
+	3	$\frac{3}{5}$

	5	
−	2	$\frac{4}{5}$

	3	$\frac{1}{4}$
−	1	$\frac{3}{4}$

Solve. Write the equations you use.

Juniper helps her dad make 3 pizzas. They put sausage on $1\frac{3}{4}$ pizzas. They leave the rest plain. How much is plain?

Zionna uses $2\frac{1}{3}$ cups of white flour and $1\frac{2}{3}$ cups of whole wheat flour to make bread. How much flour does she use in all?

Joseph practices piano for $\frac{1}{2}$ hour each day. How many hours does he practice in 7 days?

⭐ Gideon was $21\frac{1}{2}$ inches long when he was born. His sister was 2 inches shorter when she was born. How long was his sister when she was born?

4.11

Review   Match.

four hundred thousand seven	4,700
four hundred thousand seventy	40,700
four thousand seven hundred	400,007
forty thousand seventy	40,070
forty thousand seven hundred	400,070

Use the printed ruler to draw a line with the given length.

$1\frac{2}{4}$ in.

$\frac{3}{4}$ in.

$3\frac{2}{10}$ cm

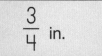

$\frac{8}{10}$ cm

Complete the boxes to find the product.

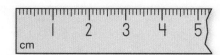

20   3

8

8 × 23 = ☐

7 × 41 = ☐

Unit Wrap-Up 👤 Connect each number to its place on the number line.

$$\frac{4}{4} \qquad \frac{1}{4} \qquad \frac{5}{4} \qquad \frac{8}{4} \qquad 1\frac{2}{4} \qquad 1\frac{3}{4}$$

0   1   2

Convert the mixed numbers to fractions.

$$2\frac{5}{6} = \boxed{\frac{}{6}}$$

$$1\frac{3}{5} = \boxed{}$$

$$3\frac{1}{4} = \boxed{}$$

$$4\frac{3}{10} = \boxed{}$$

$$6\frac{2}{3} = \boxed{}$$

$$5\frac{7}{8} = \boxed{}$$

Convert the fractions to mixed numbers.

$$\frac{8}{3} = \boxed{}$$

$$\frac{12}{4} = \boxed{}$$

$$\frac{17}{5} = \boxed{}$$

$$\frac{11}{6} = \boxed{}$$

$$\frac{17}{10} = \boxed{}$$

$$\frac{31}{8} = \boxed{}$$

Unit Wrap-Up 👤

Write a fraction to complete each equation. Then, convert the fraction to a mixed number or whole number.

$$10 \times \frac{2}{10} = \boxed{} = \boxed{}$$

$$6 \times \frac{2}{5} = \boxed{} = \boxed{}$$

Complete.

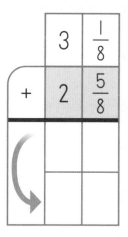

+	3	$\frac{1}{8}$
	2	$\frac{5}{8}$

+	6	$\frac{3}{4}$
		$\frac{3}{4}$

+	4	$\frac{1}{2}$
	2	$\frac{1}{2}$

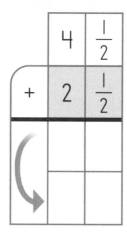
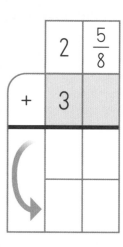

+	2	$\frac{5}{8}$
	3	

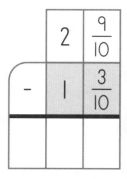

−	2	$\frac{9}{10}$
	1	$\frac{3}{10}$

−	4	$\frac{1}{5}$
	3	

−	5	
	2	$\frac{2}{5}$

−	4	$\frac{1}{3}$
	2	$\frac{2}{3}$

Solve. Write the equations you use.

Asher runs $3\frac{3}{8}$ miles. Lewis runs $1\frac{5}{8}$ miles farther than Asher.
How far does Lewis run?

Adelaide buys 4 bottles of juice.
Each bottle holds $\frac{3}{4}$ liter of juice.
How many liters of juice does she buy?

Lesson Activities

Dice Tic-Tac Toe

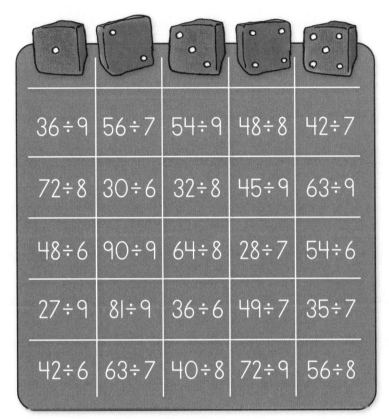

36÷9	56÷7	54÷9	48÷8	42÷7
72÷8	30÷6	32÷8	45÷9	63÷9
48÷6	90÷9	64÷8	28÷7	54÷6
27÷9	81÷9	36÷6	49÷7	35÷7
42÷6	63÷7	40÷8	72÷9	56÷8

12 ÷ 2 = ⬚   12 ÷ 3 = ⬚   12 ÷ 4 = ⬚

13 ÷ 2 = ⬚   13 ÷ 3 = ⬚   13 ÷ 4 = ⬚

14 ÷ 2 = ⬚   14 ÷ 3 = ⬚   14 ÷ 4 = ⬚

15 ÷ 2 = ⬚   15 ÷ 3 = ⬚   15 ÷ 4 = ⬚

16 ÷ 2 = ⬚   16 ÷ 3 = ⬚   16 ÷ 4 = ⬚

Possible remainders: Possible remainders: Possible remainders:

5.1

Practice — Complete.

8 [4 8]	9 [5 4]	7 [5 6]	7 [4 2]	8 [7 2]
9 [6 3]	6 [3 6]	8 [4 0]	8 [6 4]	9 [3 6]
6 [4 2]	9 [7 2]	6 [4 8]	8 [5 6]	7 [4 9]
6 [5 4]	8 [3 2]	7 [3 5]	9 [8 1]	7 [6 3]

Complete.

$25 \div 5 =$ ☐ $39 \div 10 =$ ☐ $30 \div 8 =$ ☐

$26 \div 5 =$ ☐ $40 \div 10 =$ ☐ $31 \div 8 =$ ☐

$27 \div 5 =$ ☐ $41 \div 10 =$ ☐ $32 \div 8 =$ ☐

Solve. Write the equations you use.

Abigail has a 72-inch-long board.
She cuts the board into 8 equal pieces.
How long is each piece?

There are 48 children at dance class.
The teachers divide the students into
6 equal groups.
How many children are in each group?

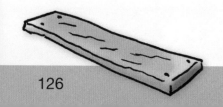

Review — Complete. Use the example to help.

Example: $1\ \dfrac{9}{8}$; $\cancel{2}\ \dfrac{1}{8}$; $-\ 1\ \dfrac{5}{8}$; $=\dfrac{4}{8}$

$4\ \dfrac{2}{6}$; $-\ 1\ \dfrac{3}{6}$

$6\ \dfrac{1}{3}$; $-\ 3\ \dfrac{2}{3}$

$5\ \dfrac{1}{4}$; $-\ 3\ \dfrac{3}{4}$

Complete the chart.

Expanded Form	Standard Form
$30{,}000 + 5$	
$30{,}000 + 50$	
$30{,}000 + 500$	
$300{,}000 + 5{,}000$	
$300{,}000 + 50{,}000$	

Complete.

$4 \times 12 = \boxed{}$ $7 \times 12 = \boxed{}$ $5 \times 12 = \boxed{}$

$9 \times 12 = \boxed{}$ $2 \times 12 = \boxed{}$ $10 \times 12 = \boxed{}$

$3 \times 12 = \boxed{}$ $8 \times 12 = \boxed{}$ $6 \times 12 = \boxed{}$

5.2

GIFT CARD
TOYS 4 YOU $30

$7

$30 ÷ 7 = [ ]

$8

$30 ÷ 8 = [ ]

$9

$30 ÷ 9 = [ ]

$12

$30 ÷ 12 = [ ]

B

Flip and Divide

Player 1		Player 2	
20 ÷ [ ]	= [ ]	20 ÷ [ ]	= [ ]
30 ÷ [ ]	= [ ]	30 ÷ [ ]	= [ ]
40 ÷ [ ]	= [ ]	40 ÷ [ ]	= [ ]
50 ÷ [ ]	= [ ]	50 ÷ [ ]	= [ ]
60 ÷ [ ]	= [ ]	60 ÷ [ ]	= [ ]
Sum of remainders	[ ]	Sum of remainders	[ ]

Practice 👤 Complete.

$49 \div 10 =$ ☐

$38 \div 5 =$ ☐

$34 \div 4 =$ ☐

$43 \div 7 =$ ☐

$39 \div 6 =$ ☐

$50 \div 8 =$ ☐

$35 \div 8 =$ ☐

$94 \div 9 =$ ☐

Solve. Write the equations you use.

Soren has 60 centimeters of yarn.
He cuts the yarn into pieces that are 8 centimeters long.
- How many pieces does he make?

Mina has 46 shells.
She puts 9 shells on each shelf.

- How many shelves does she fill?

- How much yarn is left over?

- How many shells are left over?

5.2

Review — Complete. Use the example to help.

	2	6/6
	~~3~~	
−	1	4/6
	1	2/6

	4	
−	1	4/6

	5	
−	2	1/3

	3	
−	1	4/5

Complete.

	×12
2	
4	
8	
3	
6	
9	
5	
7	
10	

Match.

kilogram   g

gram   m

liter   kg

milliliter   cm

centimeter   mL

meter   km

kilometer   L

Complete the fact family to match the marbles.

$4 \times 5 = \boxed{}$

$\boxed{} \times \boxed{} = \boxed{}$

$\boxed{} \div \boxed{} = \boxed{}$

$\boxed{} \div \boxed{} = \boxed{}$

Lesson Activities 👥

A

21 ÷ 3 = ⬚

Check: ⬚

21 ÷ 4 = ⬚

Check: ⬚

21 ÷ 2 = ⬚

Check: ⬚

21 ÷ 6 = ⬚

Check: ⬚

21 ÷ 7 = ⬚

Check: ⬚

21 ÷ 8 = ⬚

Check: ⬚

B

19 children play kickball. They make 2 teams. They make the teams as equal as possible. How many children are on each team?

19 children are at tennis practice. The coach splits them into pairs. How many pairs does he make?

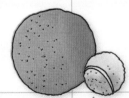

Trevor has 19 yards of fabric for costumes for the play. He needs 2 yards for each costume. If he makes as many costumes as possible, how much fabric will be left over?

⭐ 2 friends have a lemonade stand. They earn $19 and split the money equally. How much does each friend get?

Practice

Solve the division problems. Then, match them with the problem you could use to check your answer.

42 ÷ 4 = [ ]

(9 × 4) + 6

42 ÷ 8 = [ ]

(8 × 5) + 2

42 ÷ 7 = [ ]

7 × 6

42 ÷ 9 = [ ]

(4 × 10) + 2

Solve. Write the equations you use.

There are 29 children at tae kwon do lessons. They split into 3 groups and make the groups as equal as possible.
How many children are in each group?

Nikola bakes 43 cupcakes for the bake sale. He puts 6 cupcakes in each box and fills as many boxes as possible. How many cupcakes does he have left over?

38 children carpool to the nature center. 6 children fit in each minivan. How many minivans do they need to fit all the children?

Lenora arranges 45 chairs for the piano recital. She puts 8 chairs in each row. Then, she puts away the extra chairs. How many rows does she make?

Review

Complete. Use the example to help.

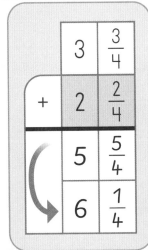

Example:

$3\frac{3}{4}$
$+\ 2\frac{2}{4}$
$=\ 5\frac{5}{4}$
$=\ 6\frac{1}{4}$

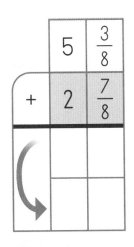

$5\frac{3}{8}$
$+\ 2\frac{7}{8}$

$4\frac{4}{5}$
$+\ 2\frac{4}{5}$

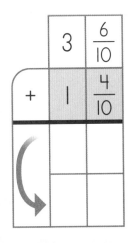

$3\frac{6}{10}$
$+\ 1\frac{4}{10}$

Connect each number to its dot on the number line.

| 249,628 | 249,130 | 250,325 | 250,050 |

249,000   250,000   251,000

| 249,500 | 249,879 | 250,501 | 250,964 |

Round each number to the underlined place. Use the number line (above) to help.

$24\underline{9},628 \approx$ ☐ $25\underline{0},325 \approx$ ☐

$24\underline{9},130 \approx$ ☐ $25\underline{0},050 \approx$ ☐

$24\underline{9},879 \approx$ ☐ $25\underline{0},964 \approx$ ☐

$24\underline{9},500 \approx$ ☐ $25\underline{0},501 \approx$ ☐

Lesson Activities

Multiplication Crash

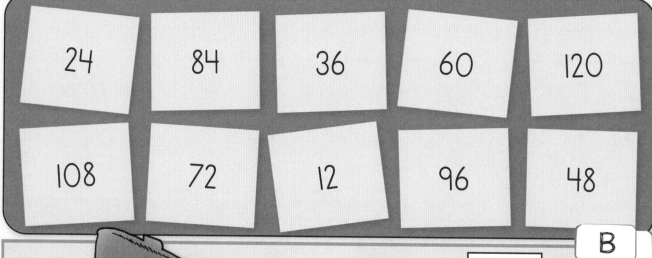

| 24 | 84 | 36 | 60 | 120 |
| 108 | 72 | 12 | 96 | 48 |

B

48 ÷ 12 = ☐

☐ × 12 = 48

24 ÷ 12 = ☐   60 ÷ 12 = ☐   120 ÷ 12 = ☐

12 ÷ 12 = ☐   108 ÷ 12 = ☐   84 ÷ 12 = ☐

36 ÷ 12 = ☐   96 ÷ 12 = ☐   72 ÷ 12 = ☐

C

55 ÷ 11 = ☐

☐ × 11 = 55

33 ÷ 11 = ☐   66 ÷ 11 = ☐   99 ÷ 11 = ☐

22 ÷ 11 = ☐   44 ÷ 11 = ☐   88 ÷ 11 = ☐

11 ÷ 11 = ☐   77 ÷ 11 = ☐   110 ÷ 11 = ☐

Practice   Complete.

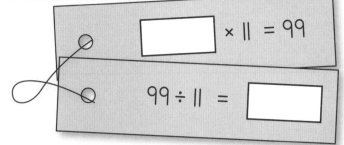

$\boxed{} \times 11 = 99$

$99 \div 11 = \boxed{}$

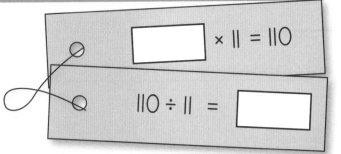

$\boxed{} \times 11 = 110$

$110 \div 11 = \boxed{}$

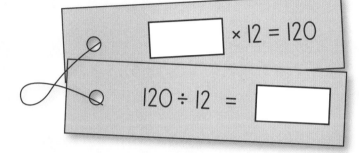

$\boxed{} \times 12 = 120$

$120 \div 12 = \boxed{}$

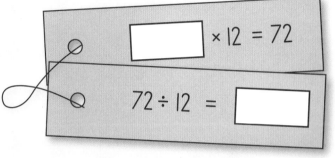

$\boxed{} \times 12 = 72$

$72 \div 12 = \boxed{}$

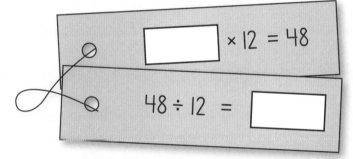

$\boxed{} \times 12 = 48$

$48 \div 12 = \boxed{}$

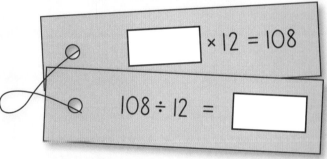

$\boxed{} \times 12 = 108$

$108 \div 12 = \boxed{}$

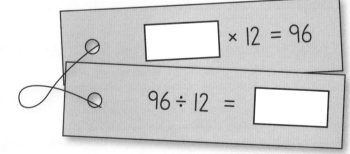

$\boxed{} \times 12 = 96$

$96 \div 12 = \boxed{}$

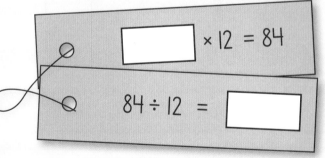

$\boxed{} \times 12 = 84$

$84 \div 12 = \boxed{}$

Solve. Write the equations you use.

Pompoms come in packs of 12.
Willow needs 60 pompoms for a craft.
How many packs should she buy?

Each movie ticket costs $11.
Charlie's dad paid $77.
How many tickets did he buy?

Review

Convert the mixed numbers to fractions. Use the example to help.

$2\frac{1}{4} = \boxed{\dfrac{9}{4}}$

$3\frac{5}{6} = \boxed{}$

$4\frac{3}{5} = \boxed{}$

Convert the fractions to mixed numbers or whole numbers. Use the example to help.

$\div \dfrac{12}{4} = \boxed{3}$

$\dfrac{15}{6} = \boxed{}$

$\dfrac{19}{8} = \boxed{}$

Complete. Follow the steps.

1. Divide
2. Multiply
3. Subtract

$9\overline{)55}$ $\qquad$ $9\overline{)65}$ $\qquad$ $9\overline{)75}$ $\qquad$ $9\overline{)85}$

Complete. All times are a.m.

10:30	30 min. → $\boxed{}$
10:40	30 min. → $\boxed{}$
10:50	30 min. → $\boxed{}$
11:00	30 min. → $\boxed{}$

Complete.

$8 \times 7 = \boxed{}$

$8 \times 70 = \boxed{}$

$8 \times 700 = \boxed{}$

$8 \times 7{,}000 = \boxed{}$

Lesson Activities 👥

A

$80 \div 4 = $ ⬜

$8 \text{ tens} \div 4 = $ ⬜ tens

$150 \div 5 = $ ⬜

$15 \text{ tens} \div 5 = $ ⬜ tens

$90 \div 3 = $ ⬜

$60 \div 2 = $ ⬜

$100 \div 5 = $ ⬜

$160 \div 8 = $ ⬜

$180 \div 6 = $ ⬜

$240 \div 4 = $ ⬜

B

MENTAL MATH ARCADE

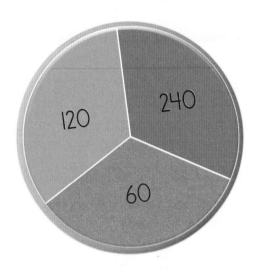

120   240   60

Candy
2 tickets

Sticker
3 tickets

Bouncy ball
6 tickets

Lollipop
10 tickets

Practice 👤 Color the problems that equal the number in the star.

20

80 ÷ 4
90 ÷ 3
60 ÷ 3

30

80 ÷ 4
60 ÷ 2
90 ÷ 3

40

80 ÷ 2
120 ÷ 3
80 ÷ 4

50

200 ÷ 2
100 ÷ 2
200 ÷ 4

Match.

180 ÷ 3	50	420 ÷ 6
320 ÷ 4	60	400 ÷ 8
210 ÷ 3	70	540 ÷ 6
250 ÷ 5	80	360 ÷ 6
360 ÷ 4	90	400 ÷ 5

Solve. Write the equations you use.

Oscar has 90 building blocks. He uses all the blocks to build 3 identical towers. How many blocks are in each tower?

Raya has 80 feet of rope. She cuts the rope into 4-foot-long pieces. How many pieces does she make?

Review

Write a fraction to complete each equation. Convert the fraction to a whole number or mixed number if possible.

$$6 \times \frac{1}{5} = \boxed{\dfrac{6}{5}} = \boxed{1\dfrac{1}{5}}$$

$$12 \times \frac{1}{4} = \boxed{} = \boxed{}$$

$$9 \times \frac{2}{10} = \boxed{} = \boxed{}$$

$$10 \times \frac{7}{10} = \boxed{} = \boxed{}$$

Match.

7 thousands	70	70 tens
7 tens	700	70 ones
7 hundreds	7,000	70 thousands
7 ten thousands	70,000	70 hundreds

Complete.

```
    6  8 , 0  9  4
 +  5  1 . 6  2  8
 _____
```

```
    6  8 , 0  9  4
 -  5  1 . 6  2  8
 _____
```

Complete.

$$(10 \times 8) + (2 \times 8) = \boxed{}$$

$$(7 \times 8) + (5 \times 8) = \boxed{}$$

$$(6 \times 8) + (6 \times 8) = \boxed{}$$

$$(8 \times 8) + (4 \times 8) = \boxed{}$$

Lesson Activities 👥

$800 \div 4 =$ ☐

8 hundreds $\div 4 =$ ☐ hundreds

$200 \div 4 =$ ☐

20 tens $\div 4 =$ ☐ tens

$400 \div 2 =$ ☐

$400 \div 4 =$ ☐

$400 \div 5 =$ ☐

$300 \div 3 =$ ☐

$300 \div 5 =$ ☐

$300 \div 6 =$ ☐

$6,000 \div 3 =$ ☐

6 thousands $\div 3 =$ ☐ thousands

$2,000 \div 4 =$ ☐

20 hundreds $\div 4 =$ ☐ hundreds

$4,000 \div 2 =$ ☐

$6,000 \div 2 =$ ☐

$8,000 \div 2 =$ ☐

$3,000 \div 5 =$ ☐

$4,000 \div 5 =$ ☐

$5,000 \div 5 =$ ☐

Flip and Divide

Player 1	Player 2
180 ÷ ☐ = ☐	180 ÷ ☐ = ☐
300 ÷ ☐ = ☐	300 ÷ ☐ = ☐
600 ÷ ☐ = ☐	600 ÷ ☐ = ☐
3,000 ÷ ☐ = ☐	3,000 ÷ ☐ = ☐
6,000 ÷ ☐ = ☐	6,000 ÷ ☐ = ☐
Sum of quotients ☐	Sum of quotients ☐

Practice 👤 Match.

2,400 ÷ 4	400	1,200 ÷ 3
800 ÷ 2	500	4,000 ÷ 8
1,000 ÷ 2	600	1,200 ÷ 2

6,000 ÷ 3	2,000	9,000 ÷ 3
15,000 ÷ 5	3,000	8,000 ÷ 2
12,000 ÷ 3	4,000	10,000 ÷ 5

Review 👤 Find the perimeter and area.

7 ft.

11 ft.

Perimeter: [   ] ft.

Area: [   ] sq. ft.

8 in.

8 in.

Perimeter: [   ] in.

Area: [   ] sq. in.

12 km

4 km

Perimeter: [   ] km

Area: [   ] sq. km

Complete with <, >, or =.

17,400 ◯ 17,004

80,000 ◯ 79,999

65,246 ◯ 56,264

108,000 ◯ 180,000

Write the time.

[   ]

[   ]

Solve. Write the equations you use.

Taylor uses 2 pieces of rope to make a rope ladder. Each piece is $4\frac{6}{10}$ m long. How much rope does he use in all?

Jude has 3 boards. He cuts each board into fourths to make steps. How many steps does he make?

Unit Wrap-Up 👤 **Match.**

55 ÷ 11	4	72 ÷ 12
77 ÷ 11	5	48 ÷ 12
88 ÷ 11	6	60 ÷ 12
44 ÷ 11	7	96 ÷ 12
66 ÷ 11	8	84 ÷ 12

Complete.

32 ÷ 8 = ☐   56 ÷ 7 = ☐

33 ÷ 8 = ☐   60 ÷ 7 = ☐

49 ÷ 7 = ☐   72 ÷ 9 = ☐

51 ÷ 7 = ☐   75 ÷ 9 = ☐

33 ÷ 6 = ☐   43 ÷ 5 = ☐

51 ÷ 5 = ☐   83 ÷ 9 = ☐

Unit Wrap-Up

Complete.

$80 \div 4 = \boxed{}$

$800 \div 4 = \boxed{}$

$8,000 \div 4 = \boxed{}$

$60 \div 2 = \boxed{}$

$600 \div 2 = \boxed{}$

$6,000 \div 2 = \boxed{}$

$240 \div 6 = \boxed{}$

$2,400 \div 6 = \boxed{}$

⭐ $24,000 \div 6 = \boxed{}$

$300 \div 5 = \boxed{}$

$3,000 \div 5 = \boxed{}$

⭐ $30,000 \div 5 = \boxed{}$

Complete.

23 people are coming for a holiday meal at McKenzee's house.
Each table seats 8 people.
How many tables do they need?

Quintin needs 6 feathers for each craft.
He has 50 feathers.
How many crafts can he make?

Rock climbing class costs $140 for 7 lessons.
How much does each lesson cost?

3 friends work together to earn $600.
They split the money equally.
How much money does each friend get?

Lesson Activities 👥

Perimeter
The distance around the outside edge

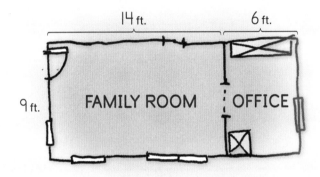

What is the perimeter of the family room?

What is the perimeter of the office?

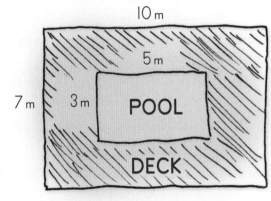

What is the perimeter of the deck?

What is the perimeter of the pool?

B

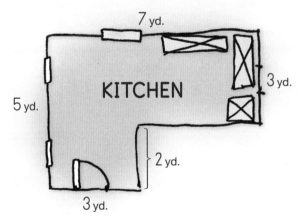

What is the perimeter of the kitchen?

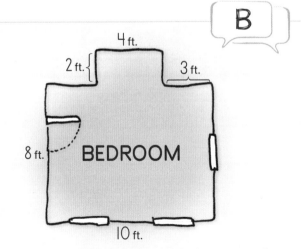

What is the perimeter of the bedroom?

Practice

Find the perimeter of each shape. Include the correct units.

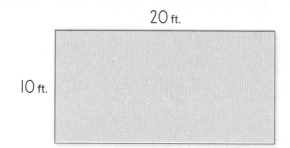

20 ft.

10 ft.

Perimeter: _____

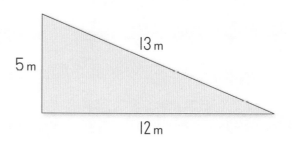

13 m

5 m

12 m

Perimeter: _____

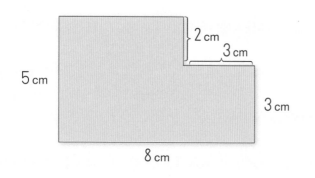

2 cm

3 cm

5 cm

3 cm

8 cm

Perimeter: _____

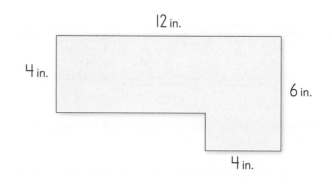

12 in.

4 in.

6 in.

4 in.

Perimeter: _____

Solve. Write the equations you use.

What is the perimeter of the tennis court?

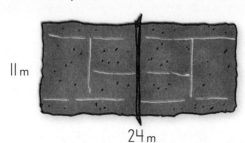

11 m

24 m

What is the perimeter of the volleyball court?

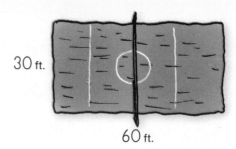

30 ft.

60 ft.

Review Complete.

	3	$\frac{4}{5}$
+	2	$\frac{2}{5}$

	5	$\frac{5}{8}$
+	2	$\frac{5}{8}$

	6	$\frac{1}{3}$
-	2	$\frac{2}{3}$

	4	$\frac{3}{10}$
-	2	$\frac{8}{10}$

Choose the more sensible unit for each item.

Weight of a feather

 1 gram   1 kilogram

Weight of a chicken

3 grams   3 kilograms

Weight of an ostrich

145 grams   145 kilograms

Complete.

$80 \div 2 = \boxed{}$ $400 \div 2 = \boxed{}$

$60 \div 3 = \boxed{}$ $320 \div 4 = \boxed{}$

$100 \div 2 = \boxed{}$ $600 \div 3 = \boxed{}$

$90 \div 3 = \boxed{}$ $640 \div 8 = \boxed{}$

Lesson Activities

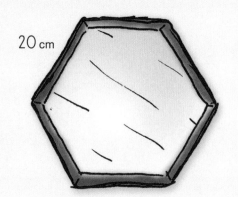

20 cm

2 Ways to Find the Perimeter of a Shape with All Equal Sides

Add up all the sides

___

Multiply the number of sides times the length of each side

40 cm

12 cm

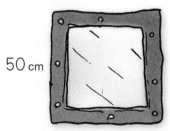

50 cm

Perimeter: ☐

Perimeter: ☐

Perimeter: ☐

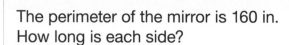

B

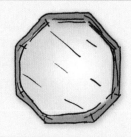

The perimeter of the mirror is 80 in. How long is each side?

The perimeter of the mirror is 60 in. How long is each side?

The perimeter of the mirror is 160 in. How long is each side?

Practice

**Find the perimeter of each shape.
All the sides of each shape are equal.**

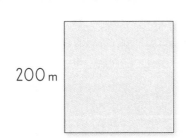

200 m

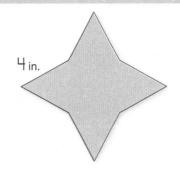

4 in.

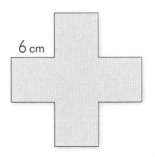

6 cm

Perimeter: [   ]   Perimeter: [   ]   Perimeter: [   ]

Complete the missing numbers in the chart.

Number of sides	Length of each side (inches)	Perimeter of shape with equal sides (inches)
6	30	
10	7	
4		24
8		160
★	20	100

Solve. Write the equations you use.

Harper makes a star craft with 10 equal sides. Each side is 6 inches long. What is the perimeter of the craft?

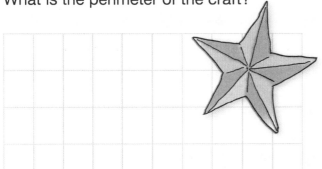

Brayden builds a garden bed with 5 equal sides. He uses 150 feet of edging to surround the bed. How long is each side?

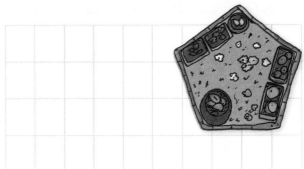

Review

Convert the mixed numbers to fractions.
Convert the fractions to whole numbers or mixed numbers.

$2\frac{7}{8}$ = ☐ $5\frac{1}{10}$ = ☐ $6\frac{5}{6}$ = ☐

$\frac{19}{6}$ = ☐ $\frac{28}{4}$ = ☐ $\frac{67}{10}$ = ☐

Complete.

$9 \times 300 =$ ☐ $9 \times 7{,}000 =$ ☐

$8 \times 700 =$ ☐ $6 \times 8{,}000 =$ ☐

$12 \times 300 =$ ☐ $11 \times 9{,}000 =$ ☐

$11 \times 400 =$ ☐ $12 \times 4{,}000 =$ ☐

$10 \times 500 =$ ☐ $10 \times 10{,}000 =$ ☐

Solve. Write the equations you use.

Poppy has 20 flowers to plant.
She plants them in 3 groups. She makes
the groups as equal as possible.
How many flowers are in each group?

Amrut's family has 2 pizzas.
They eat $1\frac{3}{8}$ pizzas.
What fraction of a pizza is left?

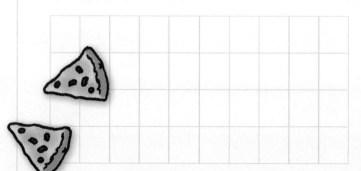

Lesson Activities 👥

LANDSCAPING HELP DESK

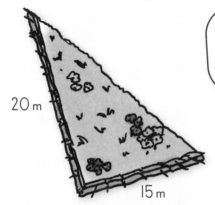

20 m

15 m

The perimeter of my yard is 60 m. I've already built a fence around 2 sides. How much more fencing do I need to fully surround the yard?

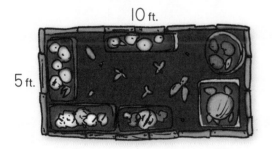

10 ft.

5 ft.

I'd like to make 3 garden beds like this one. How many feet of fence will I need to enclose all 3 beds?

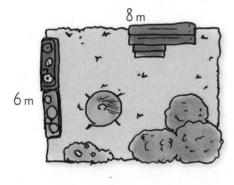

8 m

6 m

2 m

I want to build a fence around my yard. Each fence panel is 2 meters wide. How many do I need?

5 ft.

Each side of the garden is 5 feet long. I'd like to edge the garden with 1-foot bricks. Each brick costs $2. How much will it cost to buy enough bricks to enclose the garden?

Practice 👤 Find the length of the missing sides.

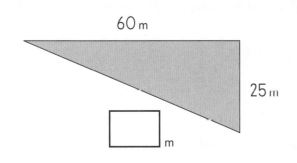

Perimeter: 150 m

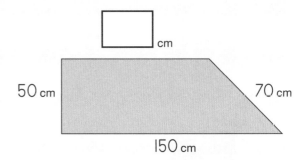

Perimeter: 370 cm

All sides are equal.

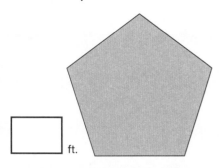

Perimeter: 40 ft.

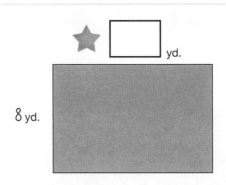

Perimeter: 40 yd.

Solve. Write the equations you use.

Porter wants to build 4 pens for chickens. Each pen is 8 feet long and 6 feet wide. How much fencing does he need?

Emilia wants to build a horse paddock 50 feet long and 40 feet wide. She already has 30 feet of fencing. How much more fencing does she need?

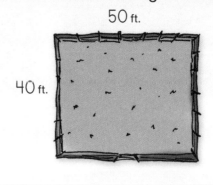

Review — Complete.

4 × 12 = ☐   8 × 12 = ☐   7 × 12 = ☐

2 × 12 = ☐   3 × 12 = ☐   10 × 12 = ☐

5 × 12 = ☐   6 × 12 = ☐   9 × 12 = ☐

Complete.

(2 × 20) + (3 × 20) = ☐

(4 × 50) + (6 × 50) = ☐

(9 × 80) + (1 × 80) = ☐

(2 × 12) + (2 × 25) = ☐

Complete. All times are p.m.

3:40 → 20 min. → 4:00

3:40 → ☐ min. → 4:10

3:40 → ☐ min. → 4:20

3:40 → ☐ min. → 4:30

Write a fraction to complete each equation. Convert the fraction to a mixed number or whole number if possible.

$4 \times \frac{3}{5} = \boxed{} = \boxed{}$ $16 \times \frac{1}{4} = \boxed{} = \boxed{}$

$30 \times \frac{1}{8} = \boxed{} = \boxed{}$ $10 \times \frac{2}{3} = \boxed{} = \boxed{}$

Lesson Activities

A

Area
The amount of space a shape covers

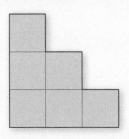

Area: [ ] sq. cm

Area of a Rectangle
length × width

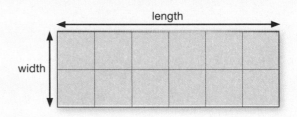

Area: [ ] sq. cm

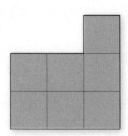

[ ] sq. cm

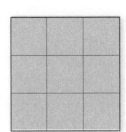

[ ] sq. cm

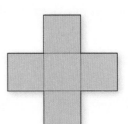

[ ] sq. cm

B

Area Capture

Player 1

Player 2

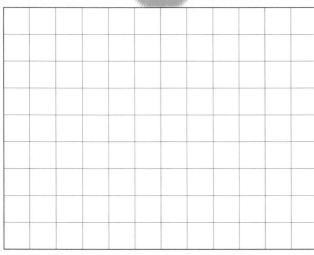

Strikes:

Strikes:

Practice Find the area of each shape.

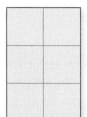 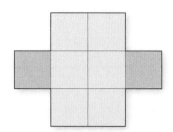 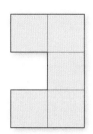

 sq. cm   ☐ sq. cm   ☐ sq. cm

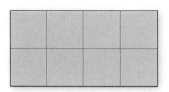 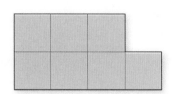 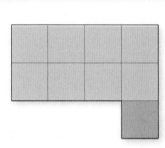

☐ sq. cm   ☐ sq. cm   ☐ sq. cm

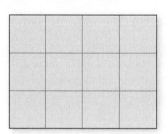 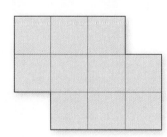 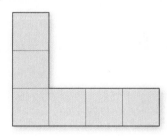

☐ sq. cm   ☐ sq. cm   ☐ sq. cm

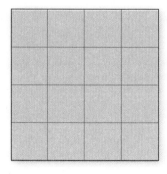 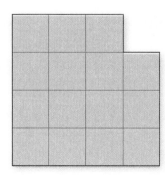 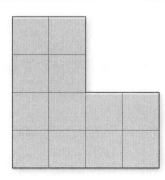

☐ sq. cm   ☐ sq. cm   ☐ sq. cm

Review   Complete the boxes to find the product.

```
        50        5
  4 [        |        ]
```
$4 \times 55 =$ [ ]

```
  [        |        ]
```
$8 \times 33 =$ [ ]

```
  [        |        ]
```
$4 \times 44 =$ [ ]

```
  [        |        ]
```
$7 \times 77 =$ [ ]

Complete. All times are p.m.

5:15	60 min. →	6:15
5:30	[ ] min. →	6:15
5:40	[ ] min. →	6:15
5:55	[ ] min. →	6:15

Round to the underlined digit.

$\underline{3},824 \approx$ [ ]

$7,\underline{6}30 \approx$ [ ]

$14\underline{7},899 \approx$ [ ]

$385,\underline{4}01 \approx$ [ ]

Complete with <, >, or =.

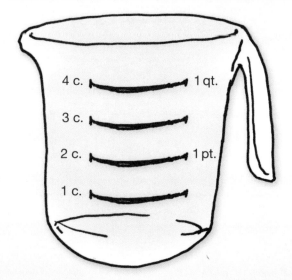

4 c. — 1 qt.
3 c.
2 c. — 1 pt.
1 c.

1 c. ◯ 1 pt.

2 c. ◯ 1 pt.

3 c. ◯ 2 pt.

4 c. ◯ 2 pt.

1 pt. ◯ 1 qt.

2 pt. ◯ 1 qt.

★ 3 pt. ◯ 2 qt.

★ 4 pt. ◯ 2 qt.

Lesson Activities 👥

Perimeter Units	Area Units
inches (in.)	square inches (sq. in.)
feet (ft.)	square feet (sq. ft.)
yards (yd.)	square yards (sq. yd.)
miles (mi.)	square miles (sq. mi.)
centimeters (cm)	square centimeters (sq. cm)
meters (m)	square meters (sq. m)
kilometers (km)	square kilometers (sq. km)

B

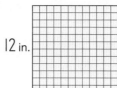

12 in.

12 in.

1 sq. ft. = _____ sq. in.

C

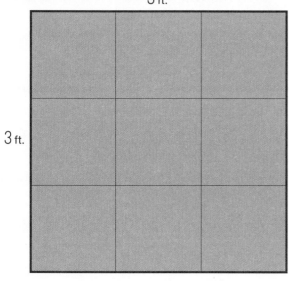

3 ft.

3 ft.

1 sq. yd. = _____ sq. ft.

100 cm

100 cm

1 sq. m = _____ sq. cm

Practice

Use the paper square foot you made in the lesson to measure the approximate area of each item.

Item	Approximate Area (Square Feet)
Television or computer screen	
Refrigerator door	
Kitchen or dining room table	
Small rug	

Find the area of each object. Include the correct units.

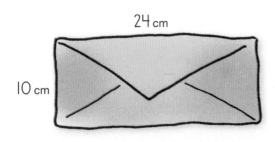

24 cm

10 cm

Area:

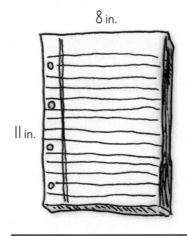

8 in.

11 in.

Area:

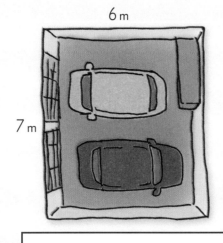

6 m

7 m

Area:

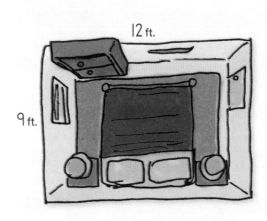

12 ft.

9 ft.

Area:

Review

Label the mixed numbers on the number line.

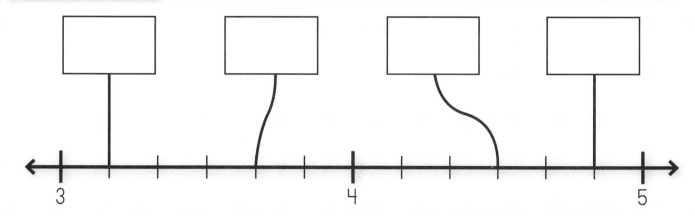

3   4   5

Complete.

$(4 \times 7) + 3 = \boxed{}$

$(6 \times 5) + 4 = \boxed{}$

$(9 \times 3) + 1 = \boxed{}$

$(6 \times 7) + 3 = \boxed{}$

$(8 \times 9) + 2 = \boxed{}$

Complete.

$36 \div 12 = \boxed{}$ $12 \div 12 = \boxed{}$

$60 \div 12 = \boxed{}$ $72 \div 12 = \boxed{}$

$24 \div 12 = \boxed{}$ $96 \div 12 = \boxed{}$

$108 \div 12 = \boxed{}$ $48 \div 12 = \boxed{}$

$84 \div 12 = \boxed{}$ $120 \div 12 = \boxed{}$

Solve. Write the equations you use.

The Fresh Loaf Bakery earned $17,864 in October. It earned $25,041 in November. How much more did it earn in November than October?

The Fresh Loaf Bakery makes 300 loaves of bread each day. How many loaves does it make each week?

Lesson Activities 👥

A

Carpet for bedroom:

Tile for kitchen:

B

Wood flooring for family room and office:

C

Wood decking for area around pool:

Practice

Find the area of the shaded part of each shape.

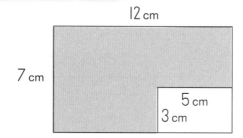

Area: ☐ sq. cm

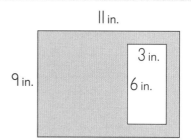

Area: ☐ sq. in.

Match each shape with the equation that tells its area.
Then, complete the equation. All measurements are in meters.

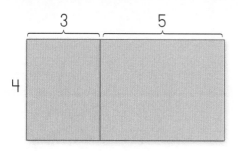

$(4 \times 5) + (2 \times 2) = \boxed{}$

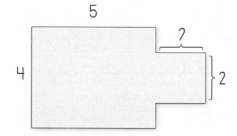

$(4 \times 4) + (2 \times 2) = \boxed{}$

$4 \times (3 + 5) = \boxed{}$

$(6 \times 5) - (2 \times 2) = \boxed{}$

Review   Complete.

44 ÷ 11 = ☐   66 ÷ 11 = ☐   33 ÷ 11 = ☐

77 ÷ 11 = ☐   88 ÷ 11 = ☐   110 ÷ 11 = ☐

55 ÷ 11 = ☐   22 ÷ 11 = ☐   99 ÷ 11 = ☐

Find the weight of each item. Include the correct unit.

Complete.

40 × 5 = ☐

400 × 5 = ☐

4,000 × 5 = ☐

60 × 8 = ☐

600 × 8 = ☐

6,000 × 8 = ☐

Solve. Write the equations you use.

Each batch of brownies requires $\frac{3}{4}$ cup of sugar.
If you make 3 batches,
how much sugar do you need?

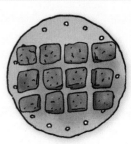

Daniel runs $\frac{4}{10}$ of a kilometer.
Miri runs 5 times as far as Daniel.
How far does Miri run?

Lesson Activities 👥

FABRIC STORE HELP DESK

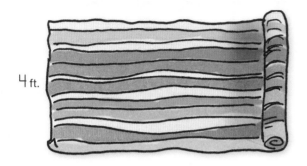

4 ft.

The striped fabric is 4 ft. wide. I need 36 sq. ft. to make a shower curtain. How long a piece should I buy?

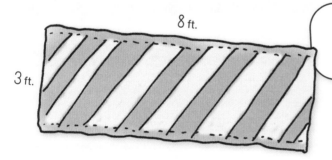

10 yd.

2 yd.

I'd like to buy this fabric to make curtains. Each square yard costs $7. How much does the fabric cost?

8 ft.

3 ft.

I'd like to cut this fabric into 4 equal pieces to make pillows. What will be the area of each piece?

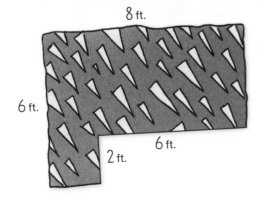

8 ft.

6 ft.

2 ft.

6 ft.

I had a piece of fabric that was 6 ft. by 8 ft. Then, I cut off a piece of fabric that was 2 ft. by 6 ft. How many square feet of fabric do I have left?

Practice 👤   Find the length of the missing sides.

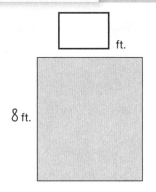

ft.

8 ft.

Area: 56 sq. ft.

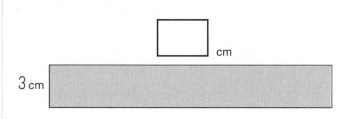

cm

3 cm

Area: 60 sq. cm

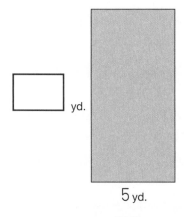

yd.

5 yd.

Area: 50 sq. yd

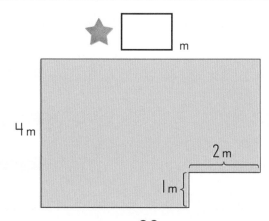

⭐ m

4 m

2 m

1 m

Area: 22 sq. m

Solve. Write the equations you use.

Owen finds an old sheet 8 ft. long and 5 ft. wide. He cuts the sheet into 4 equal pieces to make crafts. What is the area of each piece?

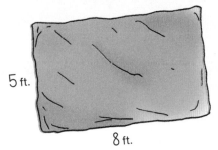

5 ft.

8 ft.

Amelia tapes together 6 sheets of paper to make a banner. Each piece of paper is 8 in. wide and 10 in. long. What is the area of the banner?

8 in.

10 in.

Review

Words	Standard Form
thirty thousand	
two hundred thousand	
nine thousand six	
fifty thousand four hundred	
four hundred thousand sixty	

Complete.

$360 \div 9 =$ ☐ $4,800 \div 6 =$ ☐

$560 \div 8 =$ ☐ $3,200 \div 8 =$ ☐

$450 \div 5 =$ ☐ $6,300 \div 7 =$ ☐

Write each length as a fraction or mixed number.

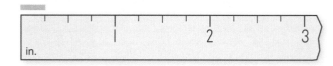

☐ in.

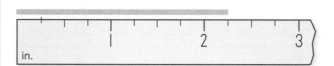

☐ in.

☐ cm

☐ cm

Unit Wrap-Up 👤 Choose the more sensible unit for each item.

Perimeter of a sticky note

20 cm	20 m

Perimeter of a window

18 in.	18 ft.

Perimeter of a garden

14 m	14 km

Area of a sticky note

25 sq. cm	25 sq. m

Area of a window

20 sq. in.	20 sq. ft.

Area of a garden

10 sq. m	10 sq. km

Find the perimeter of each shape. Include the correct unit in your answer.

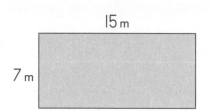

15 m
7 m

All sides are equal.

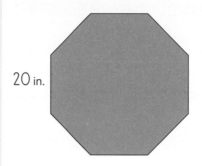

20 in.

5 ft.
3 ft. 7 ft.
8 ft.
12 ft.

Perimeter: _____   Perimeter: _____   Perimeter: _____

Unit Wrap-Up 👤

Find the area of each shape.
Include the correct unit in your answer.

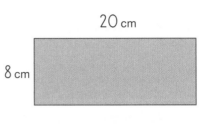

20 cm

8 cm

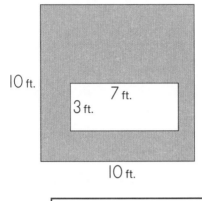

5 m

2 m

2 m   2 m   5 m

1 m

10 ft.

7 ft.

3 ft.

10 ft.

Area: _____   Area: _____   Area: _____

Find the length of each missing side.

All sides are equal.

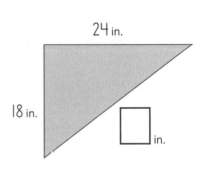

24 in.

18 in.

☐ in.

Perimeter: 72 in.

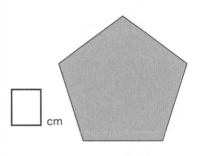

☐ cm

Perimeter: 40 cm

☐ m

6 m

Area: 42 sq. m

Use the price list and diagram to answer the questions. Write the equations you use.

PRICE LIST

Ceiling Trim............ $2 per foot
Carpet.........$4 per square foot

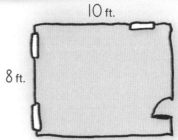

10 ft.

8 ft.

• How much will it cost to carpet the room?

• How much will it cost to put ceiling trim around the edge of the room?

7.1

Lesson Activities 👥

A

Tickets to the concert cost $21.
How much do 3 tickets cost?

```
  2 1
  2 1
+ 2 1
------
```
```
    2 1
  ×   3
------
```

```
  4 3
+ 4 3
------
```
```
    4 3
  ×   2
------
```

```
  3 2
  3 2
  3 2
+ 3 2
------
```
```
    3 2
  ×   4
------
```

B

Tickets to the game cost $24.
How much do 3 tickets cost?

```
  2 4
  2 4
+ 2 4
------
```
```
    2 4
  ×   3
------
```

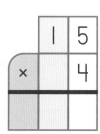

```
  1 5
  1 5
  1 5
+ 1 5
------
```
```
    1 5
  ×   4
------
```

```
  3 5
  3 5
+ 3 5
------
```
```
    3 5
  ×   3
------
```

Practice

Complete. Use the sample problem to help.

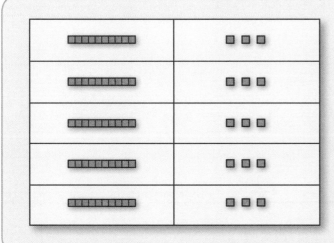

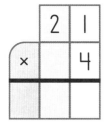

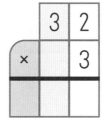

Solve. Write the equations you use.

Tickets to the hockey game cost $16.
How much does it cost to buy 6 tickets?

Khadija is 7 years old.
Her great-grandfather is 13 times her age.
How old is her great-grandfather?

7.1

Review

Find the perimeter of each shape.
All the sides of each shape are equal.

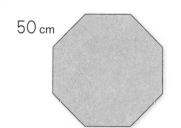

50 cm

Perimeter: ☐

7 ft.

Perimeter: ☐

8 in.

Perimeter: ☐

Complete.

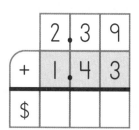

	2 .	3	9
+	1 .	4	3
$			

	3 .	8	5
-	1 .	4	0
$			

Draw a line to match.

$2\frac{3}{4}$ in.

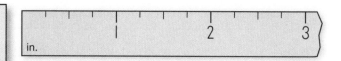

$3\frac{5}{10}$ cm

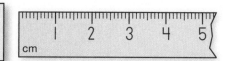

$4\frac{1}{10}$ cm

Complete.

11 × ☐ = 77

11 × ☐ = 99

11 × ☐ = 110

12 × ☐ = 24

12 × ☐ = 48

12 × ☐ = 72

12 × ☐ = 60

12 × ☐ = 96

12 × ☐ = 84

170

Lesson 7.1

Lesson Activities

A

Box Method

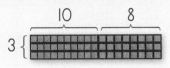

10   8

3 [   ]

3 × 18 = [   ]

30   5

7 [   ]

7 × 35 = [   ]

Algorithm

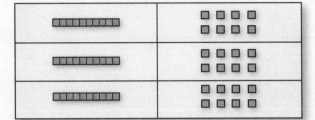

```
  1  8
×    3
─────────
```

```
  3  5
×    7
─────────
```

B

Roll and Multiply

Player 1

| 2 8 | 3 9 | 7 2 | 8 5 |

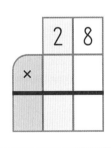 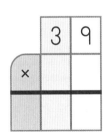 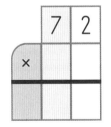

Player 2

| 2 8 | 3 9 | 7 2 | 8 5 |

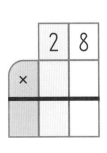

Practice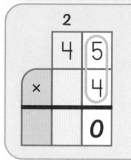

Complete.

```
      2                          2
    ┌─┬─┐                      ┌─┬─┐
    │4│5│              →       │4│5│
  ┌─┼─┼─┤                    ┌─┼─┼─┤
  │×│ │4│                    │×│ │4│
  ├─┼─┼─┤                    ├─┼─┼─┤
  │ │ │0│                    │1│8│0│
  └─┴─┴─┘                    └─┴─┴─┘
```

```
    ┌─┬─┐            ┌─┬─┐
    │9│2│            │4│8│
  ┌─┼─┼─┤          ┌─┼─┼─┤
  │×│ │2│          │×│ │5│
  ├─┼─┼─┤          ├─┼─┼─┤
  │ │ │ │          │ │ │ │
  └─┴─┴─┘          └─┴─┴─┘
```

```
    ┌─┬─┐        ┌─┬─┐        ┌─┬─┐        ┌─┬─┐
    │2│5│        │8│0│        │5│1│        │2│4│
  ┌─┼─┼─┤      ┌─┼─┼─┤      ┌─┼─┼─┤      ┌─┼─┼─┤
  │×│ │8│      │×│ │4│      │×│ │6│      │×│ │9│
  ├─┼─┼─┤      ├─┼─┼─┤      ├─┼─┼─┤      ├─┼─┼─┤
  │ │ │ │      │ │ │ │      │ │ │ │      │ │ │ │
  └─┴─┴─┘      └─┴─┴─┘      └─┴─┴─┘      └─┴─┴─┘
```

```
    ┌─┬─┐        ┌─┬─┐        ┌─┬─┐        ┌─┬─┐
    │7│1│        │6│3│        │7│5│        │1│9│
  ┌─┼─┼─┤      ┌─┼─┼─┤      ┌─┼─┼─┤      ┌─┼─┼─┤
  │×│ │8│      │×│ │3│      │×│ │4│      │×│ │7│
  ├─┼─┼─┤      ├─┼─┼─┤      ├─┼─┼─┤      ├─┼─┼─┤
  │ │ │ │      │ │ │ │      │ │ │ │      │ │ │ │
  └─┴─┴─┘      └─┴─┴─┘      └─┴─┴─┘      └─┴─┴─┘
```

Find the missing digits.

```
    ┌─┬─┐            ┌─┬─┐
    │3│6│            │7│4│
  ┌─┼─┼─┤          ┌─┼─┼─┤
  │×│ │5│          │×│ │7│
  ├─┼─┼─┤          ├─┼─┼─┤
  │1│ │0│          │5│1│ │
  └─┴─┴─┘          └─┴─┴─┘
```

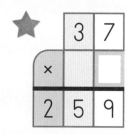
```
    ┌─┬─┐
    │3│7│
  ┌─┼─┼─┤
  │×│ │ │
  ├─┼─┼─┤
  │2│5│9│
  └─┴─┴─┘
```

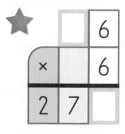
```
    ┌─┬─┐
    │ │6│
  ┌─┼─┼─┤
  │×│ │6│
  ├─┼─┼─┤
  │2│7│ │
  └─┴─┴─┘
```

Solve. Write the equations you use.

The sea lions at the zoo eat 56 kilograms of fish each week. How much fish do they eat in 4 weeks?

The elephants eat 27 bales of hay each week. How many bales of hay do they eat in 6 weeks?

Review 👤 Find the length of the missing sides.

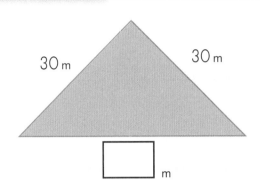

30 m   30 m

▭ m

Perimeter: 102 m

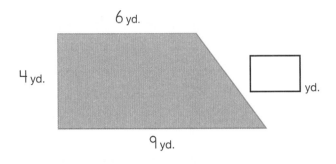

6 yd.

4 yd.

▭ yd.

9 yd.

Perimeter: 24 yd.

Label the mixed numbers on the number line.

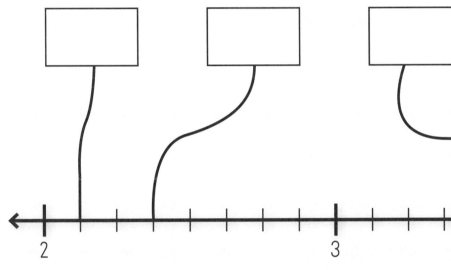

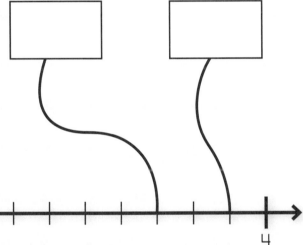

2   3   4

Solve. Write the equations you use.

Abram has 26 marshmallows.
He makes 6 cups of hot chocolate.
He puts 4 marshmallows in each cup.
How many marshmallows does he have left?

Emery makes 8 cups of hot chocolate.
She puts 3 marshmallows in each cup, and then she has 2 left.
How many marshmallows did she start with?

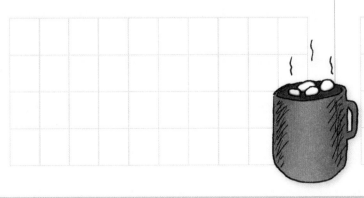

Lesson Activities

$142

How much do 3 lamps cost?

	1	4	2
×			3

How much do
3 bookshelves cost?

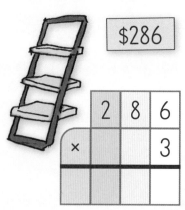

$286

	2	8	6
×			3

How much do
2 armchairs cost?

$470

	4	7	0
×			2

How much do
8 chairs cost?

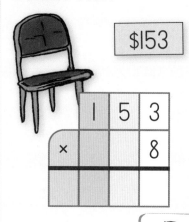

$153

	1	5	3
×			8

Snowball Fight

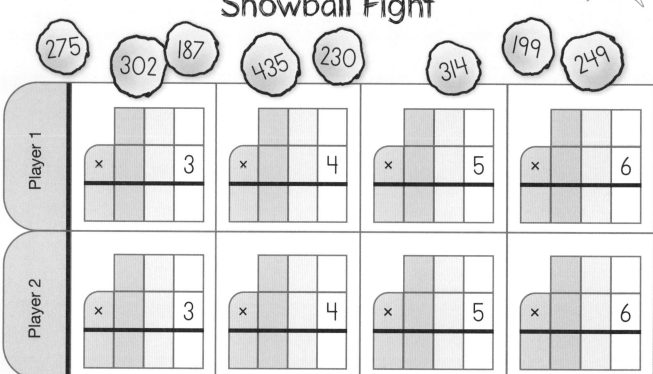

275   302   187   435   230   314   199   249

Player 1

×			3
×			4
×			5
×			6

Player 2

×			3
×			4
×			5
×			6

Practice 👤 Complete.

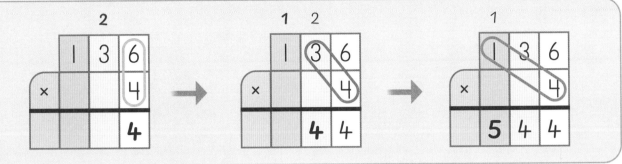

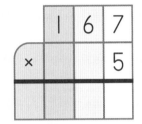

Use the price list to solve. Write the equations you use.

How much do 4 small rugs cost?

Small rug $178

Large rug............. $349

Side table $245

How much do 3 large rugs cost?

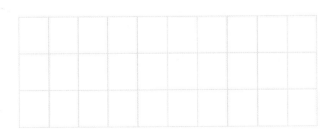

⭐ How much do 3 large rugs and 2 side tables cost?

Review

Find the length of the missing sides. All the sides of each shape are equal.

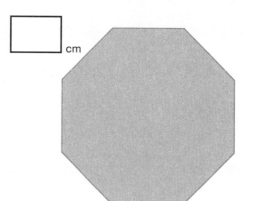

Perimeter: 120 in.

Perimeter: 400 cm

Complete.

$48 \div 6 = \boxed{}$

$480 \div 6 = \boxed{}$

$4,800 \div 6 = \boxed{}$

$48,000 \div 6 = \boxed{}$

Complete.

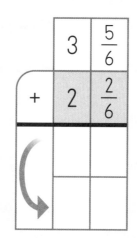

Round each number to the underlined place. Use the number line to help.

29,000   30,000   31,000

$3\underline{0},572 \approx \boxed{}$

$3\underline{0},371 \approx \boxed{}$

$2\underline{9},865 \approx \boxed{}$

$2\underline{9},099 \approx \boxed{}$

Lesson Activities 👥

Estimate

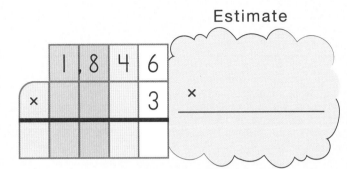

× _____

Estimate

× _____

SPIN TO WIN!

Player 1

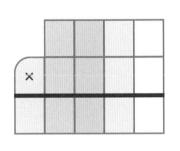

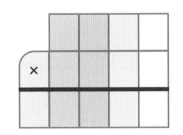

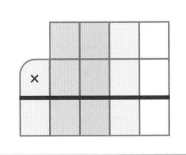

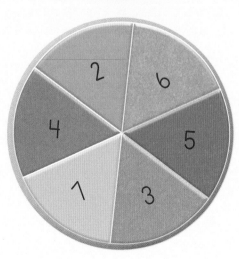

Player 2

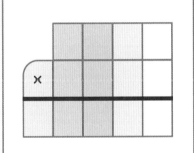

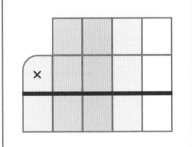

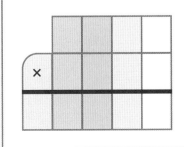

Practice

Estimate the answer to each problem. Then, solve.

Estimate

```
  6,4 5 3
×       2
```

× _____

Estimate

```
  1,7 4 1
×       3
```

× _____

Estimate

```
  2,0 6 9
×       4
```

× _____

Estimate

```
  1,3 4 0
×       5
```

× _____

Estimate

```
  2,3 0 1
×       3
```

× _____

Estimate

```
  5,1 3 8
×       4
```

× _____

Solve. Write the equations you use.

The reptiles at the zoo eat 2,300 mealworms each day. How many mealworms do they eat each week?

The tigers and lions eat 1,475 pounds of meat each month. How much meat do they eat in 6 months?

7.4

Review 👤 Match pairs whose sum is 90.

| 60 | 70 | 75 | 45 | 50 | 65 |

| 20 | 45 | 40 | 25 | 15 | 30 |

Copy the shapes.

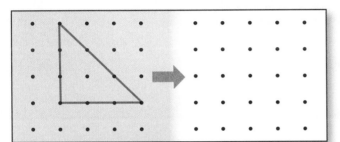

Find the perimeter and area of the shape.

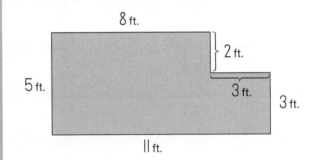

8 ft.

2 ft.

5 ft.

3 ft.

3 ft.

11 ft.

Perimeter:

Area:

Convert the mixed numbers to fractions.
Convert the fractions to mixed numbers or whole numbers.

$5\frac{2}{3} = \frac{17}{3}$

$4\frac{7}{10} = \boxed{}$

$9\frac{1}{2} = \boxed{}$

$\frac{13}{6} = 2\frac{1}{6}$

$\frac{18}{5} = \boxed{}$

$\frac{32}{8} = \boxed{}$

Lesson Activities 👥

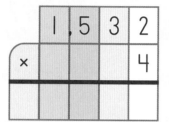

	1,	5	3	2
×				4

	2,	6	3	0
×				5

	7,	2	9	4
×				3

1,762 ft.

1,762 ft.   1,762 ft.

1,762 ft.

What is the perimeter?

	1,	7	6	2
×				4

38 cm

What is the area?

27 m

4 m

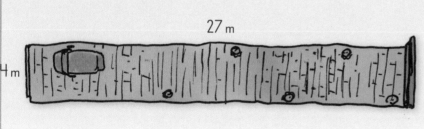

	2	7
×		4

38 ft.

9 ft.

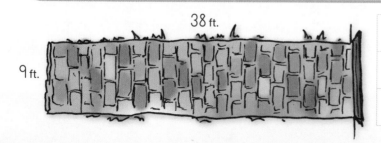

Practice 👤 Complete.

```
  1 , 5 4 6
×         3
```

```
  9 , 0 9 0
×         2
```

```
  7 , 9 6 0
×         4
```

```
  3 , 3 3 3
×         5
```

```
  3 , 0 6 2
×         7
```

```
  2 , 4 9 5
×         8
```

Use multiplication to solve. Write the equations you use.

Each side of the flag is 27 cm long. What is the perimeter of the flag?

The rose garden at the botanical garden is 9 feet wide and 137 feet long. What is its area?

Maryem helps her parents build this deck. Each square foot of decking costs $4. How much does it cost to buy enough decking to cover the whole deck?

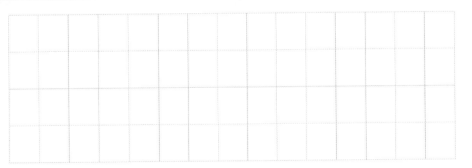

8 ft.

16 ft.

Review 👤 Match pairs whose sum is 180.

| 90 | 110 | 120 | 115 | 100 | 135 |

| 60 | 45 | 70 | 90 | 65 | 80 |

Copy the shapes.

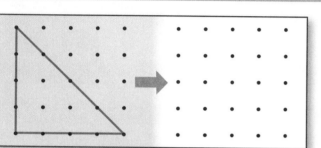

Find the shaded area.

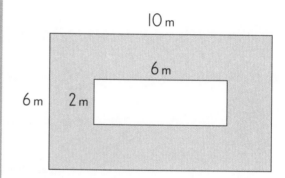

10 m

6 m

6 m   2 m

Area: _____

Use the words in the word bank to complete the blanks.

12, 24, 30, and 54 are _____ of 6.

1, 3, and 9 are _____ of 9.

15 is _____ by 1, 3, 5, and 15.

13 is a _____ number.

14 is a _____ number.

prime
○
composite
○
factors
○
multiples
○
divisible

Unit Wrap-Up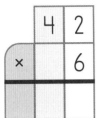

Complete.

```
    4 2
×     6
─────────
```

```
  4 0 6
×     5
─────────
```

```
  1,0 3 2
×       8
─────────
```

```
    7 8
×     5
─────────
```

```
  3 1 2
×     3
─────────
```

```
  1,3 7 0
×       7
─────────
```

```
    9 7
×     3
─────────
```

```
  2 9 1
×     4
─────────
```

```
  1,1 1 1
×       9
─────────
```

Find the area or perimeter of each shape.

All sides are equal.

34 cm

Perimeter: ☐

All sides are equal.

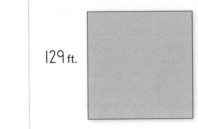

129 ft.

Perimeter: ☐

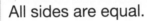

46 m

8 m

Area: ☐

Unit Wrap-Up

Use the price list to answer the questions. Write the equations you use.

	Price per round-trip ticket
Greece	$880
Costa Rica	$704
South Africa	$912
India	$1,065
Australia	$2,143
Thailand	$1,539

How much do 2 tickets to Greece cost?

How much do 5 tickets to Costa Rica cost?

How much do 3 tickets to South Africa cost?

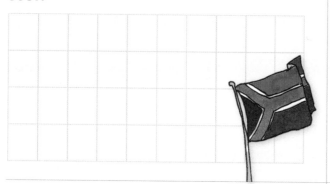

How much do 5 tickets to India cost?

How much do 6 tickets to Australia cost?

How much do 4 tickets to Thailand cost?

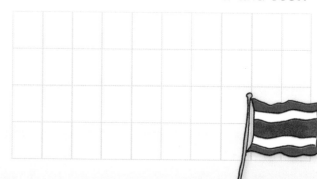

Lesson Activities 👥

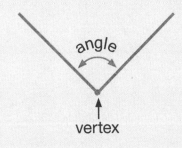

angle

vertex

An **angle** is formed when two lines meet.

The point where the lines meet is the **vertex** of the angle.

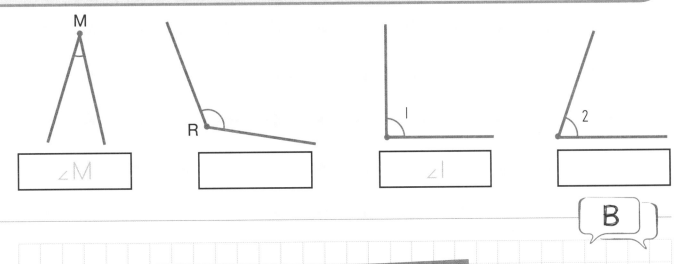

M

∠M

R

1

∠1

2

ANGLES IN MY NAME

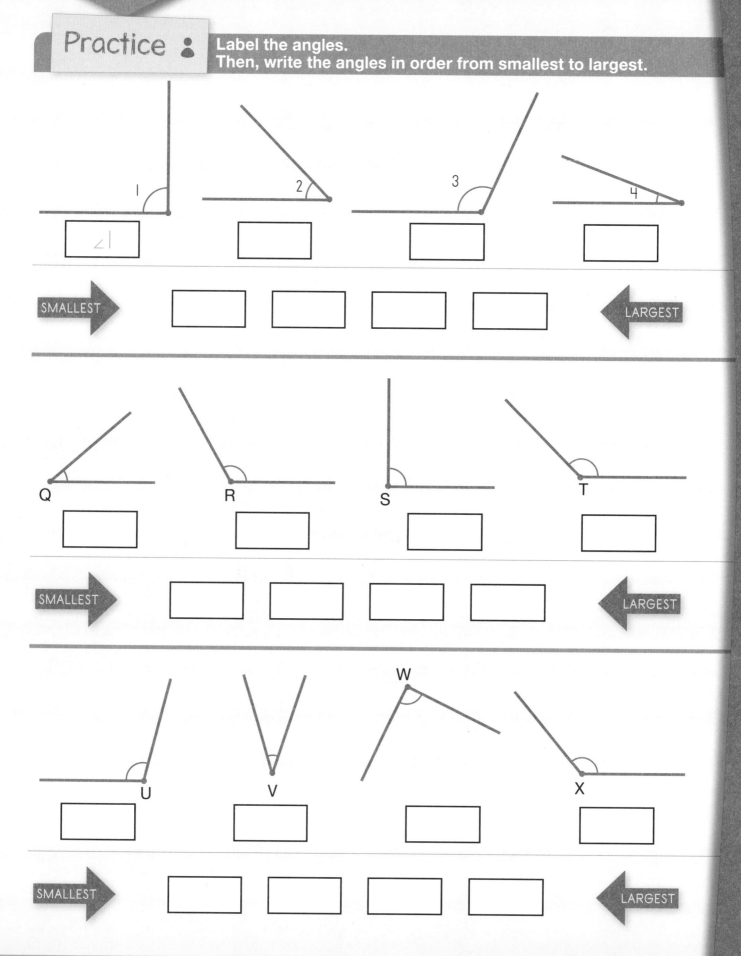

Practice

Label the angles.
Then, write the angles in order from smallest to largest.

1	2	3	4
∠1			

SMALLEST → ☐ ☐ ☐ ☐ ← LARGEST

Q	R	S	T
☐	☐	☐	☐

SMALLEST → ☐ ☐ ☐ ☐ ← LARGEST

U	V	W	X
☐	☐	☐	☐

SMALLEST → ☐ ☐ ☐ ☐ ← LARGEST

Review 👤 Complete.

	3	,	2	9	4
×					7

	1	,	5	0	4
×					9

	2	,	1	8	5
×					6

Choose the more sensible unit for each measurement.

Height of a cup

10 cm	100 m

Weight of a cup

290 g	290 kg

Capacity of a cup

175 mL	175 L

Convert the mixed numbers to fractions.
Convert the fractions to mixed numbers or whole numbers.

$7 \frac{2}{5} = \boxed{}$

$7 \frac{2}{10} = \boxed{}$

$6 \frac{2}{6} = \boxed{}$

$\frac{43}{6} = \boxed{}$

$\frac{43}{10} = \boxed{}$

$\frac{43}{8} = \boxed{}$

Solve. Write the equations you use.

Caleb has $10.00.
He buys a drink for $2.79
and a sandwich for $6.55.
How much money does
he have left?

Lesson Activities 👥

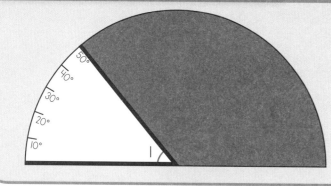

m∠1 = [   ] °

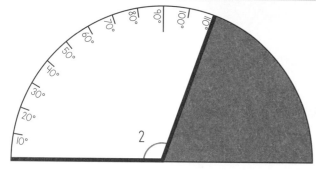

m∠2 = [   ]

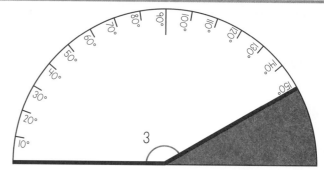

m∠3 = [   ]

Angle	∠A	∠B	∠C	∠D	∠E	∠F
Estimate						

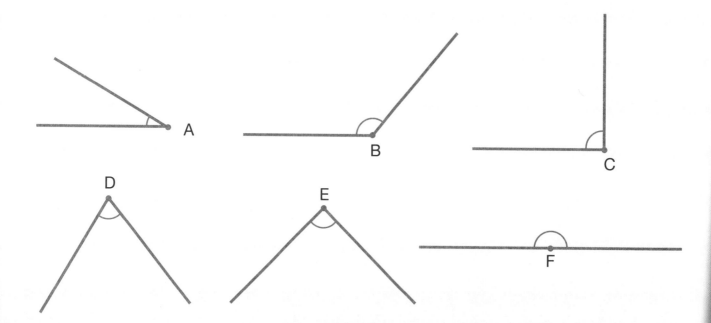

Practice 👤 Find the measure of each angle.

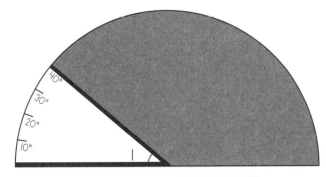

m∠1 = [＿＿＿]

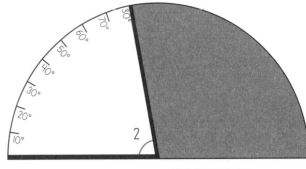

m∠2 = [＿＿＿]

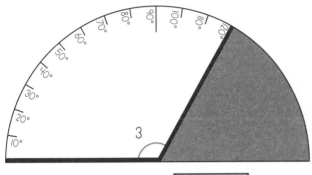

m∠3 = [＿＿＿]

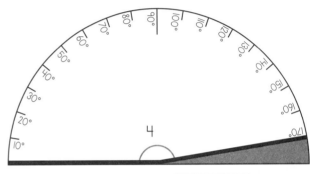

m∠4 = [＿＿＿]

Choose the more reasonable measurement for each angle.

| 20° | 120° |

| 60° | 160° |

| 40° | 90° |

| 100° | 80° |

| 180° | 140° |

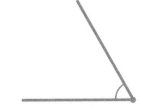

| 30° | 60° |

8.2

Review 👤 Complete.

	2	9	6
×			4

	8	3	5
×			3

	3	0	5
×			7

	9	9	9
×			6

Complete. All times are a.m.

7:55 → 15 min. → ▢

8:40 → 40 min. → ▢

9:50 → ▢ min. → 10:10

▢ ← 35 min. ← 11:30

▢ ← 60 min. ← 11:55

Complete.

150 - 35 = ▢

275 - 50 = ▢

400 - 65 = ▢

510 - 40 = ▢

820 - 60 = ▢

900 - 150 = ▢

Solve. Write the equations you use.

Mihika uses the calendar to find there are 13 weeks until the first day of spring. How many days are there until the first day of spring?

Phoenix's karate lessons cost $28 per week. How much do 4 weeks of karate lessons cost?

Lesson Activities

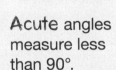

Right angles measure 90°.

Acute angles measure less than 90°.

Obtuse angles measure more than 90° and less than 180°.

Straight angles measure 180°.

Angle Four in a Row

Key

 Acute   Right   Obtuse   Straight   Wild   Remove one counter

Practice Match.

Acute

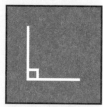

Right

Obtuse

Straight

Copy the angle. Then, write whether it is acute, right, obtuse, or straight.

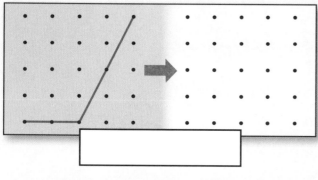

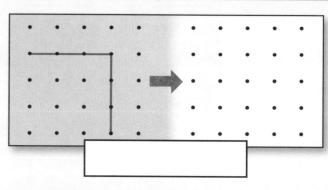

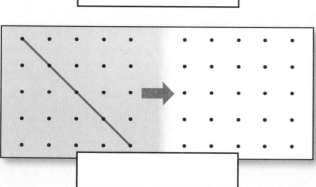

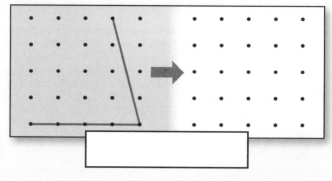

Review 👤 Complete.

	7	3
×		6

	9	8
×		6

	5	5
×		9

	8	7
×		5

	6	3
×		7

Complete. Convert your answer to a whole number or mixed number if possible.

$\dfrac{7}{8} + \dfrac{4}{8} = \boxed{} = \boxed{}$

$\dfrac{15}{6} - \dfrac{4}{6} = \boxed{} = \boxed{}$

$10 \times \dfrac{1}{5} = \boxed{} = \boxed{}$

$8 \times \dfrac{3}{4} = \boxed{} = \boxed{}$

Solve. Write the equations you use.

Samuel's family buys carpet for this room. Each square foot of carpet costs $4. How much does the carpet cost?

11 ft.

9 ft.

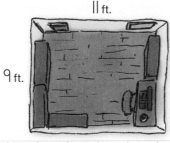

The area of this room is 96 square feet. One side of the room is 12 feet long. How long is the other side?

12 ft.

Lesson Activities 👥

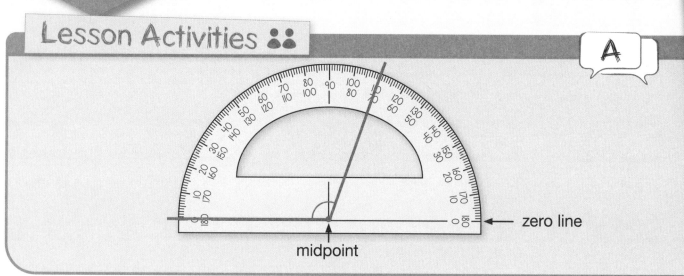

zero line

midpoint

How to Measure Angles with a Protractor

1. Line up the midpoint and vertex.
2. Line up the zero line and one side of the angle.
3. Choose the correct scale.
4. Find where the other side of the angle intersects the scale.

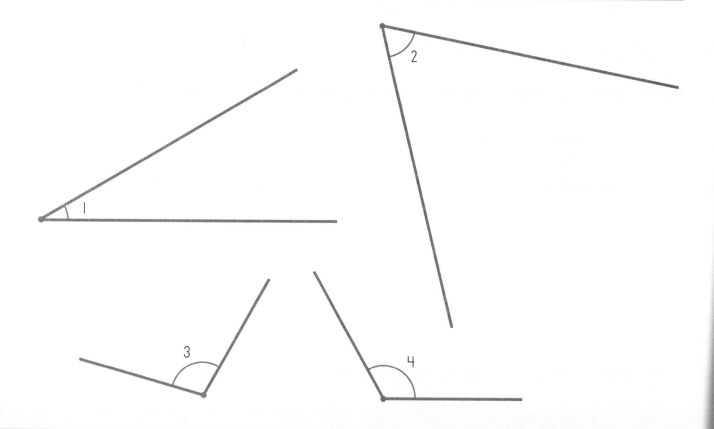

Practice   Use the printed protractor to measure the angles.

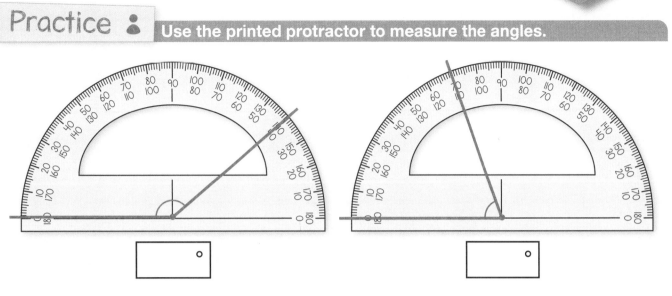

Use a real protractor to measure the angles. Extend the sides as needed.

Angle	Measure
∠ L	
∠ M	
∠ N	
∠ O	

N

O

L

M

Review

Complete.

	3,	0	7	8
×				6

	4,	2	9	0
×				5

	6,	7	0	8
×				9

Complete.

$(6 × 10) - (6 × 2) = $ ☐

$6 × (10 - 2) = $ ☐

$(6 × 5) + (6 × 3) = $ ☐

$6 × (5 + 3) = $ ☐

★ $6 × (1 + $ ☐ $) = 48$

Find the perimeter and area.

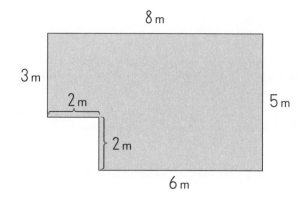

8 m

3 m

2 m

2 m

5 m

6 m

Perimeter: ☐

Area: ☐

Solve. Write the equations you use.

Apollos uses $\frac{2}{3}$ cup of brown sugar and $\frac{2}{3}$ cup of white sugar to make chocolate chip cookies.
How much sugar does he use in all?

Janessa's family has a 5 kg bag of potatoes. She helps her dad peel $2\frac{2}{10}$ kg to make a big batch of mashed potatoes.
How many kilograms of potatoes do they have left?

Lesson Activities 👥

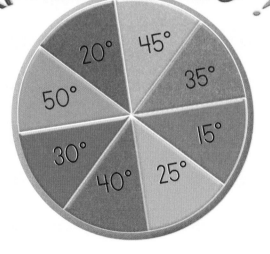

Player 1	Player 2

Practice

Use a protractor to draw an angle with the given measure. Use the printed line for one side. Use the dot for the vertex.

Review

Complete. Follow the steps.

1. Divide
2. Multiply
3. Subtract

7 | 6 5   6 | 4 5   8 | 7 5   9 | 5 5

Color the problems that match the number in the star.

 3

| 71 – 68 |
| 60 ÷ 30 |
| 36 ÷ 12 |

 4

| 96 – 91 |
| 110 – 106 |
| 48 ÷ 12 |

 7

| 63 – 56 |
| 77 ÷ 11 |
| 92 – 84 |

 9

| 108 ÷ 12 |
| 81 – 72 |
| 270 ÷ 3 |

 30

| 200 ÷ 4 |
| 210 ÷ 7 |
| 15 × 2 |

 40

| 25 × 2 |
| 200 ÷ 5 |
| 360 ÷ 9 |

 70

| 35 × 2 |
| 240 ÷ 3 |
| 210 ÷ 3 |

 90

| 720 ÷ 8 |
| 55 × 2 |
| 45 × 2 |

Solve. Write the equations you use.

Aliya walks 5 km each day. How many kilometers does she walk in 31 days?

Milo's family usually drives about 230 miles per week. How many miles do they drive in 6 weeks?

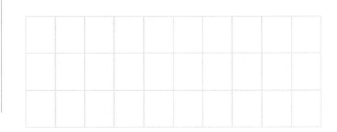

Lesson Activities 👥

Pattern Block Angles

 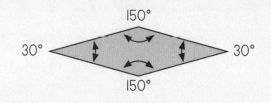 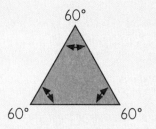

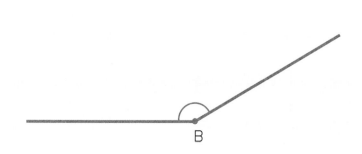

Equations

m∠ A =

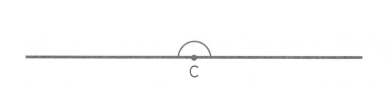

Equations

m∠ B =

Equations

m∠ C =

Practice 👤 Use the labeled angles to find the missing angle measures.

  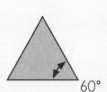 

45°   60°   30°

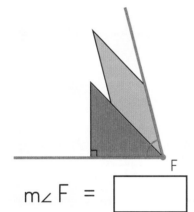

m∠ F = [   ]

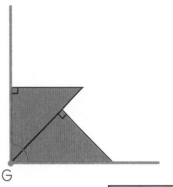
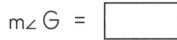

m∠ G = [   ]

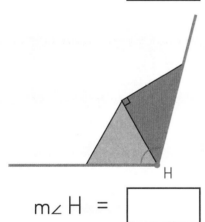

m∠ H = [   ]

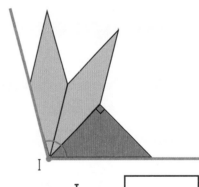

m∠ I = [   ]

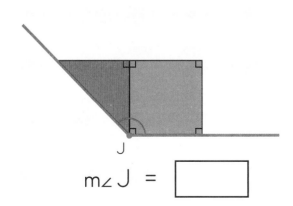

m∠ J = [   ]

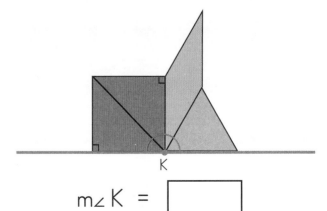

m∠ K = [   ]

Review 👤 Complete.

	8	4	5
×			7

	9	3	7
×			4

	8	2	5
×			8

	7	0	7
×			7

Write whether each angle is acute, right, obtuse, or straight.

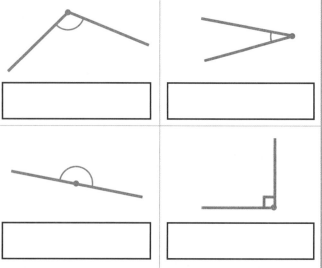

Circle the prime numbers. X the composite numbers.

15	16	17	18
19	20	21	22
23	24	25	26
27	28	29	30

Solve. Write the equations you use.

Evie sews together 5 pieces of fabric to make a blanket. Each piece of fabric is 30 in. long and 8 in. wide. What is the total area of the blanket?

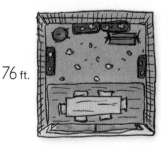

8 in.

30 in.

Eliana's backyard is shaped like a square. Each side is 76 feet long.
What is the perimeter of her yard?

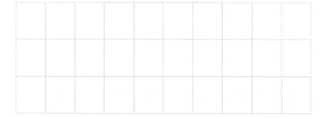

76 ft.

Lesson Activities 👥

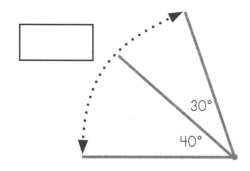

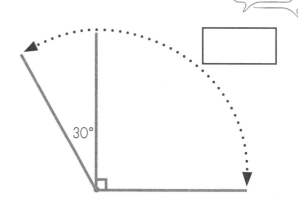

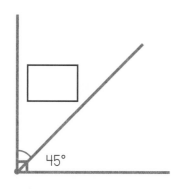

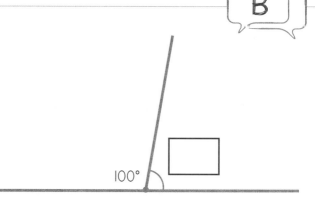

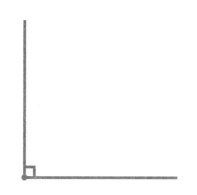

Practice 👤 **Find the missing angle measures.**

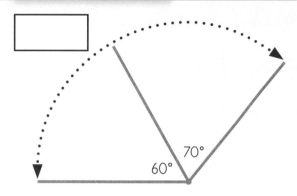

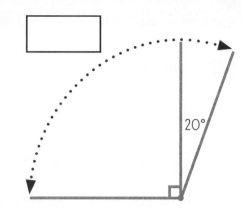

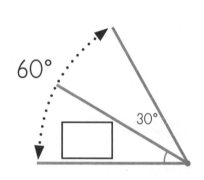

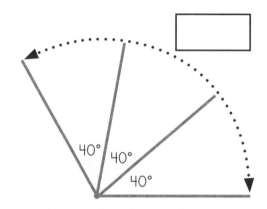

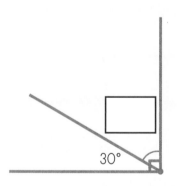

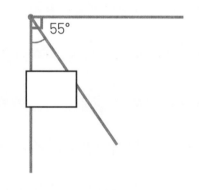

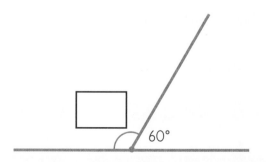

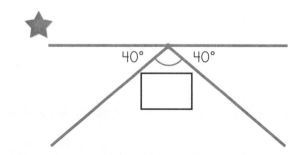

Review

Complete.

3 $\frac{1}{5}$
+ 2 $\frac{3}{5}$

7 $\frac{1}{10}$
− 4 $\frac{6}{10}$

4 $\frac{3}{8}$
+ 2 $\frac{2}{8}$

5
− 2 $\frac{5}{6}$

Use a protractor to measure the angles. Extend the sides as needed.

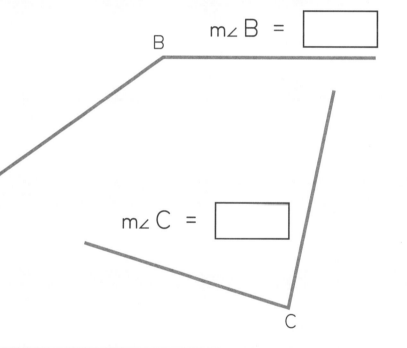

$m\angle A =$ [ ]

$m\angle B =$ [ ]

$m\angle C =$ [ ]

Solve. Write the equations you use.

Forge has 28 craft sticks.
He needs 3 sticks for each snowflake craft.
After he makes as many snowflakes
as possible, how many craft sticks will he
have left?

3 friends work together to earn $150.
They split the money equally.
How much does each friend get?

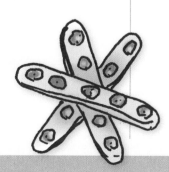

8.8

Unit Wrap-Up 👤

Choose the more reasonable measurement for each angle.

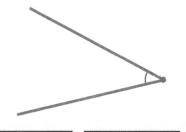  

| 40° | 80° | | 105° | 150° | | 170° | 180° |

Write whether each angle is acute, right, obtuse, or straight. Then, use a protractor to measure each angle.

Angle	∠Q	∠R	∠S	∠T
Type				
Measure				

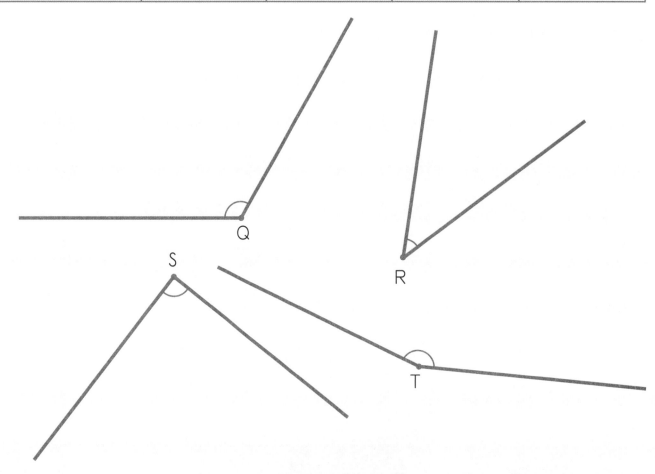

Unit Wrap-Up 👤

Use a protractor to draw an angle with the given measure. Use the printed line for one side. Use the dot for the vertex.

25° **125°**

Find the missing angle measures.

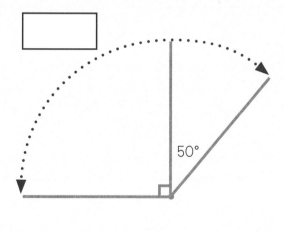

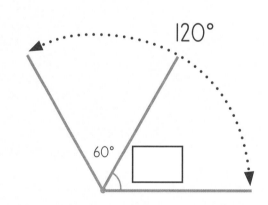
120°
60°

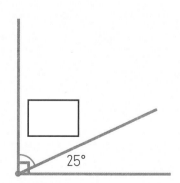
25°

⭐

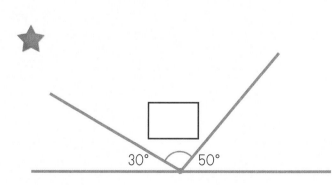
30° 50°